CHILDCARE
3-6 YEARS

KINGFISHER

PRACTICAL GUIDES

CHILDCARE 3-6 YEARS

BRIAN WARD

CONSULTANT
DR KAREN TEMPLE, MRCP

Senior Registrar in Genetics, Hospitals for Sick Children,
Great Ormond Street

Kingfisher Books

Kingfisher Books, Grisewood & Dempsey Ltd,
Elsley House, 24–30 Great Titchfield Street,
London W1P 7AD

First published in 1990 by Kingfisher Books

© Kingfisher Books 1990

BRITISH LIBRARY CATALOGUING IN
PUBLICATION DATA
Ward, Brian
    Childcare 3–6 years.
    1. Children. Home care
    I. Title   II. Temple, Karen   III. Series
    649'.1

    ISBN 0-86272-469-4

Senior Editor: Janice Lacock
Editorial Assistant: Sophie Figgis
Illustrated by Coral Mula and Mary Tomlin
Phototypeset by Southern Positives and
Negatives (SPAN), Lingfield, Surrey
Printed in Spain

CONTENTS

INTRODUCTION

Children between the ages of three to six years are a joy to be with. They are alert and enquiring, and they repay your love with their affection and interest. At the same time, they can try the patience of a saint. Because a toddler is a small person, rather than a helpless and acquiescing baby, it is tempting to treat him as a small adult. But he is not an adult, and if you treat him as such, you will soon come to think that your child is balky and unpredictable, bad tempered or overactive. Just because your child can talk to you and understand the things you tell him this does not mean that he reacts to you or his environment in an 'adult' manner.

Most of the 'problems' people experience with young children are due to lack of understanding of the child's abilities and temperament. A young child won't allow himself to be hurried, and he will make an issue of small matters that you don't consider worthy of an argument. If you are to enjoy life to the full with your child, you must understand what 'makes him tick' and become a competent though probably unqualified child psychologist.

A compromise is needed between a strict, formal upbringing and complete chaos with no rules and not much parental interest. Perhaps the worst thing you can do is to try too hard. Your anxiety and stress will transmit itself to your child and you can expect trouble. Some concerns are, of course, natural and necessary, but if you do not worry unduly when your child plays in the dirt, or falls over and grazes his knee, you will create a more relaxed environment for the whole family. You can then concentrate on the more important issues. Your child may be grubby, but he will also be self-sufficient, confident and happy. And you, as his parents, will probably be equally happy, because you have not allowed your whole life to centre on worrying about your child.

This book aims to help you by explaining how children develop physically, emotionally and mentally, and by giving practical advice on how best to assist this development and to care for your child. It is divided into sections by subject, such as Social Skills, Everyday Care and Education. The book concludes with a list of useful addresses and a comprehensive index.

To accommodate the fact that there are two sexes, we have alternated the gender of the child with each chapter. Whichever term is used, the use of 'he' or 'she' refers to children of either sex, unless specifically stated otherwise.

DEVELOPMENT MILESTONES

Physical Development

Children grow very rapidly in their first few years, but this growth rate slows during childhood. It will accelerate again at the onset of puberty. Boys are slightly taller and heavier than girls of a given age, but the differences vary widely, and the rate of growth also changes at various stages of development.

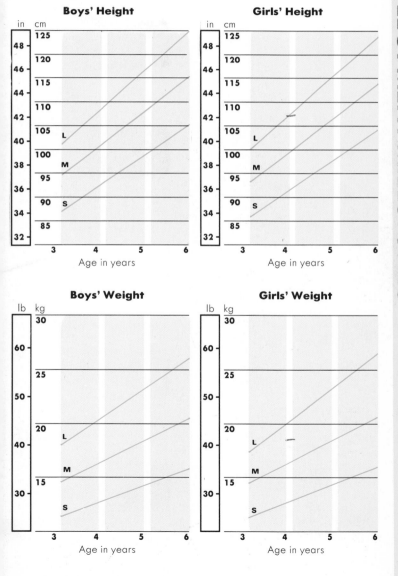

Changing proportions

In the same way, the proportions of the body alter as the child grows. At birth, the head is a quarter of the entire length of the body, but by age six it will only be one-sixth of the total length. Similarly, the legs start at about three-eighths of the total length, and become progressively longer. At adulthood, the legs are about half the length of the whole body.

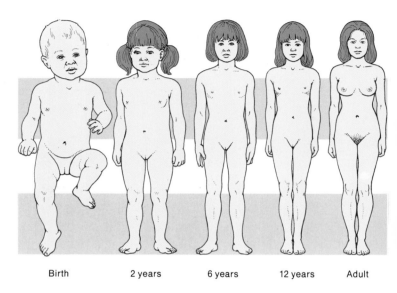

| Birth | 2 years | 6 years | 12 years | Adult |

Other physical changes also take place, and some are due to changes in fat content and its distribution in the body. This is why a chubby baby gradually slims down as he grows, even though he is steadily putting on weight.

Some physical changes are not so apparent, because different tissues and structures within the body also develop at different rates. The brain, for example, slows its development before age ten, while the sexual organs of boys and girls develop only slowly until the onset of puberty.

Developing physical skills

Many of a baby's abilities are 'pre-programmed' so that for any child they always appear in approximately the same order. Because all living creatures vary, the rate at which these skills and abilities appear also varies, so some babies walk or talk earlier or later than others.

Your toddler has a definite personality, and this can affect the rate at which he acquires new skills. For example, if he is an active child, he will spend much of his time running about and playing, so physical skills, such as kicking a ball or climbing, may be more advanced than in a child who is not so energetic.

Family background also has a strong influence here. If both parents are very active, then so too will your child enjoy lively pursuits. Any toddler mimics its parents, and your child's interests and physical skills will probably follow your own.

By age three, your toddler's physical abilities are well developed. He will be able to throw a ball, and to kick it vigorously without falling over. He can now negotiate the stairs safely, going up the stairs with one foot per step, but still going downstairs more cautiously, using both feet for each step. The age when he can confidently climb up and down stairs varies and will largely depend on his experience. If your home has many steps, he'll be confident quicker, but by four years most children can climb up and down one foot per step.

Following are some of the major physical milestones from age three to six (but always remember that they may vary widely between children).

3 years

○ Walks upstairs with alternating feet, and downstairs two feet to each step.

○ Makes a point of jumping down the last two steps.

○ Can walk backwards or sideways while playing.

○ Can stand on tiptoe.

○ Rides a tricycle.

To kick a ball in a particular direction requires good coordination and plenty of practice.

Trampolining exploits the child's developing sense of balance and, more importantly, is great fun.

4 years

○ Walks and runs up and down stairs, one foot to each step.

○ Climbs trees and ladders.

○ Sits with legs crossed.

○ Hops on one foot.

Young children enjoy testing their strength against an adult's.

As the child's agility improves so will his fondness for daredevil antics.

By five years of age, a child will be able to balance as she walks along a narrow line.

Skipping with a rope is quite a complicated manoeuvre that a child will probably master at around six years.

5 years

○ Skilful at sliding, swinging, climbing and other 'daredevil' activities.

○ Skips on alternate feet.

○ Hops on either foot.

6 years

○ Can skip with a rope.

○ Climbing frames provide an excellent form of exercise for young children as they climb and swing.

Mental reasoning

For a young child of three to six years, physical and mental abilities can be difficult to coordinate, as physical ability often exceeds the child's capacities to plan and think about his daily activities. This is why toddlers often tear about for no apparent reason, 'letting off steam' and creating uproars. He is not yet a reasoning individual, and acts unpredictably, on the spur of the moment. He is often frustrated by his inability to cope with the emotional demands of his environment and family life, so tantrums and flashes of temper will be common.

How a child interprets what he sees varies with age. In this case, a young child will only see the vegetables, whereas an older child will also make out the face.

Up until about seven years, a child will think that the more spaced out line of cotton reels contains the most reels.

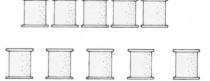

Because it looks longer, a child of six will wrongly presume that the dough on the right weighs more than that on the left.

If a child fills two identical jugs with water he knows they contain the same amount. But if he then pours the same water into different containers he will say the taller one contains more water. He understands the concept of height but not volume.

Vision, Coordination and Dextérity(손재주)능란함.

Physical strength is what gives your toddler the inexhaustable energy to run everywhere, and to keep going long past normal bedtime. But he needs to develop fine control of his physical abilities, in order to use them properly. To do this, he will need to develop a working balance between a number of abilities. He will need to coordinate his movements properly, so he doesn't fall over his own feet so often. He will use his vision in order to monitor what he is doing, and by constant repetition of everything he does, he will develop dexterity. The ball he kicks will eventually go where he aims it; he can catch the ball when it is thrown to him; the picture he draws gradually becomes recognizable.

○ Drawing requires both concentration and coordination.

These improved abilities are not solely a result of practice, but also reflect the continuing development of his nervous system. Until his brain has developed sufficiently, no amount of practice would allow a three-year-old to juggle, even though he may have adequate strength. Because the brain develops in a predictable way, he will continue to develop his fine control of movement in a particular sequence, although the times at which he reaches the various milestones will vary between children just as much as do all the other abilities.

At age three, his coordination is now good enough for him to draw laborious circles, and build quite large edifices with building blocks. He will be showing a messy interest in painting, can recognize a few colours, and will also attempt to draw a man, rarely getting further than a 'face'.

By age four, his control over coordination is much better. Now he can cut along a straight line with scissors, and he may be able to lace his shoes properly. His drawing skills are improving, and his 'man' is much more recognizable. He can identify a few letters of the alphabet, and is more discriminating about colours.

The five-year-old continues this development. His drawings of a man now have arms and legs, and he can draw a house with a door, windows and chimneys, although the perspective is still rather odd. He can colour pictures, usually staying within the outline, and now recognizes a wide range of different colours.

By six years, his drawing abilities are quite advanced. He will now draw accurate geometric shapes, and has no difficulty in recognizing and describing the differences between objects.

A three-year-old's paintings will look decidedly abstract.

She will have the dexterity to use a pair of scissors for cutting out.

3 years

- ○ Grips pencil between thumb and first two fingers.

- ○ Draws shaky circles and crosses.

- ○ Draws an incomplete 'man', comprising a round face and eyes, and some other parts of the body.

- ○ Recognizes and names most colours.

- ○ Enjoys 'painting', but sloshes colour all over the paper.

- ○ Can build a tower of up to nine blocks.

- ○ Catches a ball between outstretched hands (sometimes!).

- ○ Cuts with scissors (be careful!).

A child's early drawings will probably be representations of human faces. This example was drawn by a three-year-old.

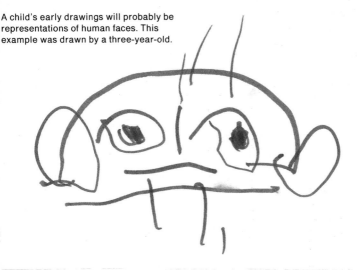

4 years

- ○ Threads small beads to make necklaces.

- ○ Grasps pencil confidently.

- ○ Draws a man showing head, body and limbs.

- ○ Draws a cross.

By five years of age manual dexterity will be developed enough to allow him to make complicated models.

Also at five years, a child will draw houses including such features as windows, doors and chimneys.

5 years

○ Builds complex models, such as steps, with building blocks.

○ Threads needle and sews stitches.

○ Matches 10–12 colours.

○ Copies simple geometric shapes, such as triangles.

○ Copies letters. Can draw some unprompted.

○ Colours pictures, staying within outline.

○ Draws man with all limbs, feet, hands etc.

○ Draws house with doors, windows and chimneys.

○ Counts on fingers.

6 years

○ Copies geometric shapes, such as diamonds, accurately.

○ Can describe visual differences between similar objects.

○ Draws a ladder.

In this three-year-old's drawing the person is shown with a head, and a trunk that extends into a leg and foot, but the emphasis is on inordinately long arms.

This portrait, drawn by a four-year-old, features all the main body parts, including individual fingers, as well as decorative buttons on the trunk. The letters are an attempt to write the name of the model.

Children's paintings reveal how they view the world. In this five-year-old's landscape, the sky and sun is shown at the top and the figures and house stand on the ground. Between the two is a void as the child thinks the two don't meet.

Children often draw activities that they see going on around them everyday. Here a six-year-old has drawn a woman cooking. She holds spoons in her hands and is standing near the cooker.

The Development of Language Skills

Like other forms of development, a child's ability to learn and use language are dependent upon the continuing development of his brain, as well as by mimicry, and constant repetition. The increasing complexity of his brain allows him to acquire language skills in a distinct order of priority, but he needs to exercise these skills constantly in order to refine his abilities. The constant chatter of a young child may seem pointless to an adult, but it is this rehearsal of newly acquired words and phrases which leads to fluency later on.

Language milestones

The three-year-old has a poor grasp of grammar, and frequently mispronounces words. But he does have some control over his voice. He can speak quietly or shout, though he never seems to do either at the appropriate time. His grasp of language is constantly being improved by listening intently to his favourite stories. He may repeat these back, chattering to himself continually while playing.

By age four his language skills are markedly improved, and he pronounces most words properly. He is able to repeat back his name, address and age, and drives adults mad with continual questions – though he seldom waits around for long enough to hear the answers. Unfamiliar words interest him, and he will ask their meaning. It is difficult for him to distinguish fact from fantasy, and he loves to hear long and involved stories. He will also make these up for himself.

The five-year-old acquires skills in singing, and takes delight in repeating rhymes and TV jingles endlessly. He still confuses a few basic sounds, but his speech is now generally clear and fluent. A grasp of difficult abstract concepts increases his general comprehension of the world about him, and he now begins to act out his fantasy stories with friends.

At six, he is able to cope with complicated descriptions and can recognize and name most of the letters of the alphabet. He is now able to utilize his language skills as a tool which will allow him to learn at school.

If you are worried that your child is behind with his speech, first remember that there is tremendous variation in the rate at which children's language skills develop. Children being taught two languages can be a little delayed initially, but they usually catch up and then have an advantage over other children.

Language is obviously closely tied in with hearing, and hearing is one of the areas your doctor will check first if your child has a speech problem (see p.145). Do contact your health visitor or doctor if you are worried.

The following verbal milestones are only rough guides to achievements by different ages so don't be alarmed if your child's development doesn't tally exactly.

3 years

○ Enjoys favourite stories.

○ Has control over pitch and loudness of voice.

○ Growing vocabulary, but usually mispronounced. Can be understood by strangers.

○ Can name himself and describe his sex.

○ Talks to himself continuously while playing.

○ Asks constant questions; usually doesn't wait for answers.

○ Repeats nursery rhymes.

○ Memorizes numbers, but does not understand quantities greater than three or four.

4 years

○ Talks fluently, with an understanding of grammar and asks for explanation of unfamiliar words.

○ Can repeat name, age and address.

○ Enjoys hearing long and rambling stories.

○ Makes up his own stories.

○ Often confuses fact with fantasy.

○ Understands simple jokes.

○ Sings simple songs.

5 years

○ Speaks fluently but still confuses sounds like f, s and th.

○ Enjoys riddles and jokes.

○ Understands abstract expressions and words.

○ Makes up 'plays' with friends.

6 years

○ Memorizes and repeats back complete sentences.

○ Uses several sentences to describe an object or situation.

○ Recognizes and names at least 20 letters of the alphabet.

○ Finger rhymes and action songs allow a child to show off language and communication skills.

Emotional and Social Development

Emotional and social development are what will convert an unruly toddler into a 'civilized' person who can take part fully in the family life, and can be trusted to behave reasonably at play group, school or with his friends.

This form of development balances the acquisition of a number of physical and mental skills with his recognition and acceptance of many unwritten rules of society.

○ Young children should be encouraged to share their toys. Although shared activities may inspire rivalry as well as cooperation.

At age three, the toddler is eager to please, and tries to help around the home. He is beginning to grasp the concept of sharing when he starts to play with other children. He also begins to understand the concept of patience, and realizes that he cannot always have things immediately, but may be asked to wait. He is affectionate towards older brothers and sisters, but becomes tearful when they do not let him play with them.

The growing confidence of the four-year-old often causes him to squabble with other children, and together with his increasing independence, make him boasting and cocky. He will often answer back or defy his parents. At this stage his mind is overactive, so his thoughts are disordered and his conversation confusing. He is able to devise games of great complexity, but is prone to lose interest and switch his attention rapidly to something else. He is extremely untidy and does not understand the need to clear up after him.

By age five, he begins to settle down a little, and seems ready to carry out small tasks without supervision. This means that he can dress himself, and wash and clean his teeth (but he still needs checking to make sure he has done things properly). He is now able to understand the need to comfort and protect his friends and pets.

The six-year-old often becomes unruly again, being stubborn and willing to use his new language skills to argue back. He is aggressive in play, needing to win all the time, and still crying in frustration if he cannot succeed. Counterbalancing this is his greatly increased ability to care for himself, developing good table manners, tying shoelaces, and completing his own dressing.

3 years

○ Can pull down pants and pull them up again after using potty.

○ Dresses and undresses, but needs help with fastenings.

○ Affectionate and confiding.

○ Tries to help adults by imitation of their activities.

○ May be dry during both day and night (but not necessarily).

○ Invents imaginary friends and invents own games.

○ Begins to share when playing with other children.

○ Understands the difference between present, past and future.

○ Beginning to learn patience.

At three years of age a child can dress herself and cope with velcro fastenings on her shoes.

By four years she will be able to wash and dry her hands thoroughly.

4 years

○ Cleans teeth.

○ Washes own hands and dries them.

○ Enjoys 'dressing up' games.

○ Invents 'construction' games.

○ Very untidy.

○ Often answers back.

○ Enjoys companionship of other children, but often argumentative with them.

○ Shows concern and sympathy when other children are upset or hurt.

5 years

○ Understands need for order, but is generally very untidy.

○ Uses knife and fork efficiently.

○ Chooses own friends.

○ Shows understanding of fair play in games.

○ Aware of clock time.

○ Protective towards pets and young children.

6 years

○ Cuts own meat and other tough foods with knife and fork.

○ Reasonably 'civilized' table behaviour.

○ Ties shoelaces.

○ Manages complicated fastenings on clothes.

○ Does not yet reason in an abstract way.

Most five-year-olds can eat efficiently using a knife and fork, but not necessarily terribly neatly.

One of the most complicated dressing skills to be mastered is tying shoelaces, achieved at about six years.

SOCIAL SKILLS

Learning Social Skills

Social development is a long process which will continue right through your child's teens, but the years between her third and sixth birthdays cover some particularly important stages in this process. At this time you can exert a strong influence on your child. Once she is at school, a whole new group of influences will come to bear, and you will be sharing your child with the educational system and a group of new friends who assume ever-increasing importance to her.

Her subsequent behaviour, and to some extent her personality, will be shaped by her parents, while she is still easily influenced by them. For these first few years, she will look up to you, because in her eyes, you can do no wrong.

Making friends

From quite an early age, your child will have taken an interest in other children, watching them and often copying their play. At first, she will be content with simply being near other children, playing alongside them, but making only tentative approaches.

Sometime in her third year, she will begin to get the idea of cooperating and sharing with others. Up to this point, her life has been largely self-centred. She has developed her own form of play, with its own rules, and even when you play with her, you follow her lead (although you will often suggest novel games for her to try). She has little concept of sharing or cooperation with others, and regards her toys as private possessions, which should be protected from other children.

These attitudes make obstacles to making friends, and it is unrealistic to expect your toddler to suddenly begin to cooperate with other young children, without a few tears and tantrums. She has spent three years learning the 'rules of the house' that you have laid down, but now she has to learn all over again, from other children who will not be as understanding and tolerant as her own parents.

She will snatch a sweet away from another child, because it seems as though this child is depriving her of the sweet. Similarly, she will not see the need to share her toys with others, and will see no reason why she should not grab their toys whenever she feels like it. Cooperative social behaviour takes a while to develop, and snatched toys and scratches or bites will be commonplace for a while.

Young children get on far better if they have a shared objective, and they usually find it easiest to cooperate in boisterous games, rather than sitting down quietly together to play. In games involving running, or kicking or throwing a ball, it soon becomes apparent to a small child that it is much more fun

Playing games with her family will give a child confidence when it comes to meeting and playing with other children.

when others are involved. Often you can initiate the game, heading off potential squabbles, and then gradually leaving them to it once they have begun to enjoy themselves. You will still need to keep an eye on their play, in case trouble develops, but try to do this inconspicuously, rather than standing there like a policeman, waiting to chastise any child who dares to upset your own child. She won't ever develop a sense of fairness if you automatically support her in every dispute with other children, and it is often best to leave them to sort it out, provided they don't become too rough.

Don't be surprised if a happy game suddenly deteriorates into tears, because it will take a long time before your child learns to cope with social interactions in an 'adult' manner. Similarly, don't get cross if one of her new friends bites or kicks (or if your own child does the same). This sort of behaviour is all part of the inability to cope with social situations, and is a sign of frustration rather than spitefulness. Of course, you must take care to separate or distract children before any real damage is done.

Young children have almost no common sense when it comes to rough play. They do not appreciate that it is dangerous to push someone when they are climbing up the ladder to a slide, or that poking someone with a stick could injure an eye. This is the primary reason why games need to be supervised, and distractions provided when things get out of hand.

It takes a while before a child realizes that the kick or pinch she administers to other children so as to get her own way hurts her just as much when another child does it back to her. When this lesson has been learned, it won't be long before a sense of 'fair play' develops in her games. You can help her by teaching her how to cooperate with others, such as explaining when it is someone else's turn to be 'it'. Another influence on her behaviour will be the actions of her new friends. If her behaviour is out of line, they will not be inhibited in letting her know, so she must rapidly learn to adjust her behaviour.

The way in which a child integrates with other children will be influenced by the way you have handled her. If you have treated her with kid gloves, rushing to comfort her after every knock, she will find the rough and tumble of making friends very difficult. In this case, she will appear shy and uncertain, hanging around the periphery of the group, and only joining in the quieter games. On the other hand, if your child is too boisterous, she may not be welcomed as a friend by other children. If you see that she is having problems, you may need to explain what is expected of her, to help make her acceptable to a group of new friends.

Making special friends

After this boisterous stage, she will usually attach herself to a special friend, with whom she will cooperate in inventing complicated games, often involving dressing up. This is the start of true friendship. She will have someone of her own age to confide in when you have annoyed her, and she will no longer feel intimidated or overawed by adults who can always insist that she does things their way. At first, boys and girls form close friendships and play well together, but by age five or six, they usually begin to shift into single-sex groups. This is probably an unconscious imitation of the behaviour of older children, who are generally scathing about the opposite sex.

Don't forget that you cannot truly choose her friends. Just like adults, children pick and choose their friends, and some children just don't get on well together. You might feel that some children are not suitable friends, because you don't like their behaviour. You must ask yourself why, before you deprive her of their friendship. Because you may not like their parents, or may disapprove of their behaviour, you could be depriving your own child of an important part of her growing up.

Young children can only make proper friendships with others who are very close to their own age. If you introduce your child to a group of older children, she will be firmly excluded from their games, or at best, barely tolerated. Similarly, however well behaved your child may be, she will be unable to resist the temptation to bully or take over a group of younger children.

Once you can trust your child to play happily with her friends, you can congratulate yourself. You and she together have passed the first hurdle of encouraging her to become an independent individual, with a mind of her own. She will still be heavily influenced by you for years to come, but will be increasingly influenced by her circle of friends, which will grow rapidly once she goes to school.

Getting on with your new baby

When you first tell your small child that there is a new baby on the way, of course she's going to be jealous. There is no point in convincing yourself that if you explain it properly, your beautifully brought-up child will happily accept the new situation, because she probably won't. Unfortunately it is impossible to predict how she will react. She may appear to accept the situation, while being secretly worried and upset, so her behaviour towards you will change. Her reaction will to some extent depend on her personality. If she is an active, outgoing child, she may become naughty or destructive; if she is naturally quiet, she may become withdrawn. Or she may appear to take it all in her stride, bottling up her feelings but showing some telltale signs of changes in her behaviour, like becoming clingy, or reverting to bed-wetting.

You are going to have to look for the areas which disturb her the most, and take steps to rectify them. If she feels that the baby is going to get all the loving, then you must be extra affectionate towards her. Bear in mind that a small child will fasten onto a poorly understood passing remark and build this up in her mind into a real problem. A remark like "We'll have a tiny new baby to play with" she might misinterpret as a direct threat from the new baby towards her favourite toys. Or a poorly coded 'private' conversation with your partner about the new baby could be understood by your child as a deliberate attempt to exclude her from the discussion (which it actually is).

The birth of a second baby is always a traumatic time for all of the family, and mothers in particular tend to be preoccupied with the new baby. Because of this, the role of the father is particularly important at this time, and you should make sure that your child does not feel neglected by both parents. With a little forethought, you can help her through the difficult time that *she* will soon experience, and make the baby's arrival seem an excitement rather than a threat. The following guidelines may help.

Get her used to the idea of a new baby Don't just spring the idea of a new brother or sister on her without warning. Prepare the ground by drawing her attention to other people's babies, and explain to her that most families have several children, and that they all get on well together. Give her plenty of time to get used to this idea before you tell her that your new baby is on the way, but make sure that no one else tells her first.

Make her feel independent Concentrate on encouraging her to do things for herself – then pretend to be surprised and pleased that she can do them. This will encourage her to feel independent and important. She may even be slightly contemptuous of the helplessness of the new baby who can't dress herself, wash her own hands, go to the toilet, etc.

○ Involving an older sister in caring for her newborn brother is a good way to avoid feelings of jealousy.

Don't brush aside her curiosity She will constantly ask you questions about the baby, so tell her everything she is capable of understanding. Don't be embarrassed about going into details – young children are incapable of sexual embarrassment. Let her feel your stomach, explain how the baby got there, and tell her how helpless it will be at first, so she knows that for a while, your attention will be mainly focused on the baby. There is no point in telling her about a future playmate, because she has little concept of 'future' and therefore will only be disappointed at the helplessness of the new baby, and won't understand why she can't play with it right away.

Prepare her for the birth Make sure that she understands what is going to happen. She needs to know that mummy will be going into hospital for a few days, so take her along on an antenatal visit so she can get used to the idea. Make sure she knows who is going to look after her, and have a trial run so she can be sure that things are not going to change too drastically while you are in hospital. Above all, don't ever let her think she is being pushed to one side because she is in the way.

Keep her involved Make sure she knows what is happening, and keep her informed and involved from the moment labour starts. Don't let her wake in the middle of the night and find you both gone; wake her briefly to say goodbye, give her a kiss and tell her when she can come to see you in hospital. That way, she won't feel that you have abandoned her.

Let her visit you in hospital as soon as possible, and make a big fuss of her as soon as she appears. Some hospitals are un-enthusiastic about allowing small children to visit, but unless there are good medical grounds for this attitude, you should insist on the visit for the good of all the family.

However careful you are to prepare your child for the new arrival, any child between the ages of three to six will experience some pangs of jealousy. It's only natural. From being the apple of your eye, able to command your sole attention, she now gets at most only half of your time, and probably far less, because babies are more labour-intensive. As soon as you get back from hospital, she wants your entire attention, or even more than usual, and she will have only a passing interest in the baby.

If you are breast-feeding, you should be tactful about feeding for the first few days. Explain to her how babies are fed, and that she herself fed from your breast before you let her see you feeding the new baby. She will probably be resentful at your closeness with the baby, and many young children will want to try sucking for themselves. Let her, if it doesn't bother you. Otherwise just let her taste a drop of milk on your finger, and tell her that you have to save the rest for the baby. Most children soon lose interest in breast-feeding once they realize it is a regular event.

You can do several things to let your child know that you understand her feelings about the baby:

Maintain her former routine Make a point of continuing to do all the activities she was involved in before the birth, as far as possible. If things have to change, to suit the new baby, explain to her why you are altering mealtimes, or having an afternoon rest, so she knows she has not upset you.

Indulge her in babyish behaviour If she sees you fussing over the new baby the same way as you used to fuss her, she will naturally feel that she is missing out. If she wants extra cuddles, a squirt of baby shampoo on her hair, or the simplest of nursery rhymes – fine, let her have her own way, and she'll soon get bored with it. Having experimented, she will be able to tell herself that she's much too grown-up for that sort of thing.

Encourage her independence If she wants to help, let her, but don't be surprised if she suddenly finds much more important things to do. Whatever you do, don't allow her to think that it is her job to help you care for the baby, or she *will* come to resent the interference with her play. With a bit of tact, you can build up her self-importance, pointing out all the things she can do because she is grown-up, unlike the helpless baby. Your partner can help here, taking her out and giving her lots of attention while you care for the baby – but be sure that she doesn't feel you are shoving her out of the way.

Remember that she is still very immature Don't expect too much of a young child. She won't react to your baby in the same way as an adult, and you can't rely on her to be responsible. So don't leave a young child alone with your baby, either indoors or in the garden, or there could be one of those upsetting accidentally-on-purpose accidents where the cot or buggy gets tipped over. It's always better to anticipate the effects of jealousy than be upset by an apparently spiteful act from a loved child.

Getting on with older brothers and sisters

A child may be jealous of a new baby, while at the same time envying older children, because of their greater freedom to do all the things she would like to try. She looks up to older children, because they are capable, physically larger, and are obviously more independent of their parents. In short, they get away with lots of the things she would like to do herself.

You can help to make her more comfortable with older children by pointing out to her the freedom she has just by virtue of being younger. After all, she doesn't have to get up early to go to school, or wear a tie or a smart dress when you have visitors. On the other hand, it's not so easy to explain to her why she has to go to bed early, or why she can't watch some television programmes, when her older siblings have this freedom.

A lot of the problems arise because of the differences in age. Older children can be cruelly dismissive of their younger brothers or sisters, deliberately excluding them from their games. Sometimes they may physically bully them, or tease and provoke them in less obvious ways. This is upsetting, because it is natural to want and expect all the family to get on well together. Unfortunately, it is rare for brothers and sisters to grow up without constant jockeying for attention and superiority. This seems to be a basic aspect of human nature in even the most loving families. The most that you can do is to be supporting and understanding, always trying to see the point of view of all of the children.

Probably the most difficult position for a young child is to be trapped between older brothers and sisters and the arrival of a new baby. This way, she gets the worst of all possible worlds, and some children can become very withdrawn in this situation. Try to find activities which can involve the whole family, so none of your children feel excluded.

Learning to take turns when playing is an important part of a child's social development.

Development of independence

The influence of other children (peer group pressure, to use the psychologists' term) will mean that you are no longer the only role model for your child to copy. Your child will pick up habits and sayings from her friends which may disturb or upset you, but you have to accept that this is all part of her growing up.

If you think that her behaviour is deteriorating unacceptably, you may wish to influence her choice of friends, but this will probably cause defiant confrontations and tantrums. It is wisest to explain to her carefully that although her friend may say or do a particular thing, this is not acceptable in *your* household. And you can also point out ways in which she is allowed to do things which are forbidden to her friend, to make the point that there are differences in the 'house rules'. Bedtime and television watching are particular causes of complaint once a child has started to mix with others.

The development of independence is a difficult time for parents, and it is easy to become exasperated with an unruly child. However, the rewards are great. The child has the satisfaction of being able to take some control of her own life, while you will have more freedom, because she will be less dependent on your constant care.

Learning the Social Graces

Between ages three to six, your child is intensely curious and exploratory, and part of her exploration is to find out the rules and permitted limits of her social life. She will be constantly testing you to see what she is allowed to do. If "No" is the answer, she will try someone else to see if she can get her own way. After a while, she will have established in her own mind what are the limits of acceptable behaviour, but at first, these will only be related to your immediate family. So although you may think she behaves quite reasonably at home, when she is with someone else, such as at a party, she may run riot, behaving unacceptably, because she is testing out the rules under these new conditions.

Don't worry too much. With a little firmness and consistency in your response, she will become more reasonable in her behaviour, although you can expect episodes of defiance as she tests out her growing independence.

Acting as policeman

At this stage in the development of your child, it is easy to find yourself constantly saying "No!", especially as many children are quite destructive. Don't worry about this, but always act with two principles in mind. Firstly, consistency is vital. Don't let yourself be worn down into letting her have her own way, if there are good reasons for checking her. You must be absolutely consistent, otherwise she will become confused about what is expected of her. There is no point in telling her off for misbehaviour on one day, then letting her do the same thing a day later, without comment. In the same way, if you want her to stop doing something you must tell her to stop with conviction, and make sure that she really does stop, or your attempts at discipline lose all credibility. Secondly, make sure you reward her for 'good' behaviour. This does not mean filling her up with rewarding tidbits like a performing dog, but simply letting her know that you are aware that she is acting responsibly.

Testing authority

Don't let your child fool you. Even at three, nearly all children know that picking your nose in front of visitors is not acceptable behaviour; neither is spitting, swinging on the curtains, or other forms of disruptive behaviour. These are all forms of 'showing off', designed to test you out when your child thinks you may not react as forcibly as usual. Don't let her get away with it, just because you are embarrassed to make a scene, but let her know that you will deal with her later. And make sure you do it.

This all sounds very negative, as though the only way to bring up your child is to constantly check her when she is naughty. That is only half of the story, because it is equally important to reward her and treat her as a responsible person when she does behave responsibly. The alternatives are to become harassed and ineffectual, resigning yourself to having your home life disrupted and watching your child's behaviour deteriorate as she gets older and grows away from you.

The parents of an only child may need to encourage him to join in with other children if he is not to become too dependent on his parents.

The only child

Being an only child can be difficult. Only children are relatively easy to care for from the parents' point of view, because they are less influenced by older brothers and sisters than children in large families. Similarly, the older child does not experience the jealousy that affects most young children when a younger brother or sister arrives.

Parents usually find only children quite easy to raise, because they are not usually influenced very strongly by other children, and so are more reliant upon their parents. The lack of brothers and sisters can make it more difficult for her to make friends, and when she reaches school age, she may be withdrawn or quiet, compared to her rowdier classmates.

Up until age three or thereabouts, the social development of an only child is no different from that of a child with brothers or sisters, because up until this stage she will not make friends or be influenced by other children to any great extent. But as she gets older, it is very important that the only child develops relationships with children of about her own age, as in an exclusively adult environment she will feel out of her depth and inadequate. However well-meaning her parents are, they cannot compensate for the rough-and-tumble of a group of young children, neither can they invent the involved and spontaneous play-acting games which are an important part of early development.

If you have an only child, you must be aware of the possible difficulties she will face. You will need to make special efforts to

○ An only child will spend a lot of time alone, so it is important to help her cultivate outside friendships.

help her to make friends, encouraging her to bring her friends back to the house or allowing her to visit them, so she can form close relationships.

There is nothing wrong with being an only child. After all, the first child in any family is an only child for a while. But if she remains alone, all the attention of the family is focused upon her, and they are likely to become overprotective and anxious. This attitude has an effect on the child too, and parents of an only child need to make special efforts to allow her to develop her full independence.

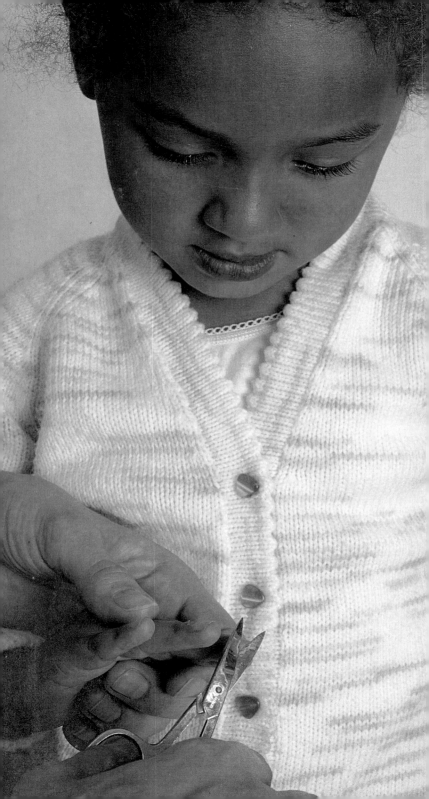

EVERYDAY CARE

Civilized Eating

Most young children fall into one of two groups when it comes to eating. On the one hand, you have the energetic child who races about all day and stops running merely to gobble down whatever you put in front of him, usually very messily, and on the other is the child who never seems to eat anything at all, and requires continual coaxing from his parents in order to get what seems to be an adequate amount of food down him. With both types of child, it is difficult to develop what an adult would accept as reasonable table manners, and you are lucky if you can avoid food being strewn about at each mealtime.

Most of the real difficulties arising at the table are due to the parents' attempt to persuade the child to do something that doesn't suit him. If you try to slow down a child who is an enthusiastic eater, you could spoil his enjoyment of food and produce eating problems. On the other hand, if he is a picky eater, your anxiety about his every mouthful will be recognized, and he will soon come to regard every mealtime as a battle of wills with you. Food then becomes the hated cause of the strife between you, and that attitude won't do a lot for his appetite.

In fact, your concerns over his apparent under-eating are almost certainly groundless, as a child will usually eat exactly the right amount of food to suit his own metabolism – remember that not all people utilize their food intake in the same way, so some need more or less than others. Provided your child gains weight at the proper rate (see p.9), and doesn't eat too much stodge or sweetened junk food, don't worry too much about how he eats.

Learning table manners

The key to encouraging civilized mealtimes is to remember that a child always learns by example. If your table manners are lacking, then you can't really expect your child to behave any better. The following points may help:

Teach him a sense of time and place Adults don't need to be told when to behave a little more formally than usual; when you have friends or relatives to a meal, or when going to a restaurant. If you want your child to respond in the same way, you will have to explain to him why this meal is 'different', and what is expected of him. If you expect your child to cope with this sort of situation, it may be worth accustoming him to the traditional 'Sunday lunch', as well as ordinary meals which out of necessity are much more casual.

Set a good example If you eat peas from a spoon, put your elbows on the table, and drink spilled tea from a saucer, you can't

If a child is to eat neatly she needs to sit at the right height for the table. A booster seat that straps onto a full-size chair will raise her to a suitable position. An apron will protect her clothes from the inevitable spillages.

reasonably expect your child to behave any differently. He will learn from your example, and speedily realize that he is the odd one out if he is behaving differently from the rest of the family.

Encourage experimentation Most young children are extremely suspicious of any new food, and never seem to tire of favourites like sausages and beans, every single day if they get the chance. Obviously they need a balanced diet, and you should encourage your child to eat as wide a range of foods as possible.

If he thinks that you are going to try to force him to eat a whole plateful of something unfamiliar, you can expect a disturbed mealtime. It's far better to use a little psychology. You can offer him a small taste while you are cooking, and leave it to him to ask for some. Or better still, give him his usual meal, and eat the new dish yourself, making a show of how much you have enjoyed it. He will almost certainly want to try it, especially if you look doubtful and suggest that "it's really for grown-ups".

It is also very easy for a parent's prejudices to be carried over to the children. Just because you may not like fish, spinach or mushrooms, there is no reason to deny them to your child. He may devour them without comment, provided you don't let him know that you dislike them yourself. Alternatively, a diet of raw carrot, cabbage and boiled lentils may be very good for him but if you are not prepared to eat it why should he?

Give him time Although some children gobble their food down as fast as possible so they can get back to their play, others take little apparent interest in eating. They may sit and daydream, and sometimes even forget to chew and swallow when they have a mouthful of food. You can remind them that they should be hurrying things along, but don't nag them too much, or they will often decide that they never really wanted that particular meal anyway, and just lose interest.

On the other hand, don't leave your child sitting for too long looking at a rapidly cooling and progressively more unappetizing meal, which he obviously is never going to eat. If you try and force him to eat when he isn't in the mood, or just doesn't like what you have prepared, he could come to expect every meal to be an ordeal or a punishment. It's far better to take away the offending dish and leave the meal for a while.

Keep it simple It's natural to take pride in preparing good meals, but you must be careful not to overload a young child with too many unusual tastes and textures. It's far better to give him familiar meals with perhaps one new item on the plate, than to present him with an elaborate meal full of suspicious-looking items, each of which has to be tasted and considered.

Treat him like a grown-up So long as your child is in a high chair, and has to wear a bib, he will behave like a toddler at mealtimes, throwing food about and getting it on himself. Once he is in (or on) a proper chair he will feel like a proper member of the family, and begin to behave as you do at mealtimes, especially when he is able to discard his baby knife and fork and eat with the same cutlery as yourself.

Don't be inhibited about taking a young child into a restaurant. Though you may be afraid that he will create an embarrassing disturbance (and of course sometimes he will), most restaurants are used to this, and will probably tuck you away in an inconspicuous corner. Even if the restaurant serves highly spiced food that you don't think he will enjoy, most menus contain something children will like, and he will probably be tempted to taste what you are eating.

Sitting pretty Almost all children go through a phase of wandering around during mealtimes, or leaving the table and then wanting to come back a little later. It's up to you how you handle this. You will have to think about what causes this kind of behaviour. It could be because he has quickly bolted down his first course, and become bored while waiting for you to finish so the next course can be served. If so, why not give it to him now? Perhaps there is something on the television that he can half-see, so he wanders off with a piece of toast in order to eat while watching? It's easy enough to switch the television off, though it may cause tears and tantrums. Perhaps he's just not hungry? Or is his portion too big for him to finish, so he has got fed up with staring at it?

All sorts of reasons can cause him to get down from the table before you have all finished. If it only happens occasionally, forget it. But if this is a regular feature of his life, you had better try and rectify the situation if you ever want to have civilized mealtimes again.

○ With practice managing cutlery becomes second nature to children and they become adept at eating all kinds of food.

Eating For Health

When it comes to eating, children definitely lack sophistication and subtlety. Though it may make you cringe to see dollops of tomato ketchup splashed all over almost all meals, or huge quantities of baked beans being devoured, almost all children like these foods because they appeal to their sense of taste. Children tend to enjoy sweet flavours and salty tastes, so they like almost all sweetened foods, together with salty snacks like crisps. Most children are doubtful about sour tastes and definitely dislike bitter tastes like coffee. Obviously there are exceptions, and most children gradually change their preferences as they get older.

Producing healthy meals need not be time-consuming or expensive – a boiled egg with bread fingers forms a nutritious, quick meal.

The dangers of too much sugar and salt

Unfortunately, sweet and salty foods are not good for you, or for your child, except in small amounts, and it is not sensible to allow your child to become too dependent on 'junk foods' which contain very large amounts of sugar and salt. And it's not only junk foods which are the culprits, because most of the so-called convenience foods available in shops are also very high in these substances.

So try not to get your child too dependent on sweets, sticky buns and heavily sweetened drinks. Sugar is the biggest problem, because it can be bad for a child in two ways. Just as with adults, too much sugar leads to overweight, and if your child has too much sugar he won't be just chubby, he will be *fat*. A bigger problem is the bad effect of sugar on the teeth. Excess sugar has been shown to lead to dental decay, and this problem is discussed in more detail on pp.50–52.

Sweets are obviously the worst culprit as a source of sugar, and they are doubly dangerous to the teeth because they are sticky and in contact with the teeth for a long time. Many older people automatically give children large numbers of sweets, using them as a reward or bribe for good behaviour, or to comfort them when they are upset. This is definitely not a good idea, and will certainly lead to later dental problems. It is difficult to resist giving sweets to your child if you have plenty of them about, or if you eat them yourself. It is easiest to avoid the issue by not having sweets in the house at all, and giving them to your child only as an *occasional* special treat, but never letting them become an automatic snack item.

Don't allow a child to have sweets before bedtime either. Brushing teeth is rarely an efficient process at this age and the sugar will stay in contact with the teeth for hours.

You will probably feel you are depriving your child of one of life's pleasures. Not at all. He can have fruit, nuts, dried fruit, cheese and any number of other snacks as a substitute. Better still, he can eat these whenever he likes, as long as he doesn't eat so much that he spoils his appetite.

Planning a healthy diet
As we have seen, it is very difficult to dictate to a child what he should or should not eat, but it is worthwhile encouraging healthy eating. There are a few guidelines to healthy eating which should prove useful.

Your child's body needs a variety of nutrients to grow: protein provides the building blocks of tissues; fat and carbohydrate provide energy; and vitamins and minerals are essential for the complicated pathways of the body. These nutrients are provided by different food groups.

Foods that are high in protein, which is vital for building cells and muscles, include meat, poultry, fish and pulses.

Cereals such as bread, pasta and rice are high in carbohydrates, which generate energy. Wholemeal cereals are best.

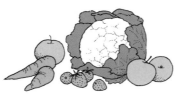

Fruit and vegetables are particularly valuable for growing children as they contain fibre, minerals and vitamins.

Milk and milk products such as yogurt and cheese are an important source of energy as well as calcium.

You should use a combination of these groups in each meal. In addition fatty foods, such as butter, margarine, chocolate, chips and cakes, can be given in moderation. A pint of milk a day (whole milk if under five years) is good for a growing child.

Iron is essential for the formation of blood cells so it is a good idea to include foods that are high in iron in a child's diet. Examples include red meat, turkey, chicken, egg yolk, lentils, chick peas and green vegetables. Vitamin C helps the body absorb iron so add oranges or tomatoes to the diet.

Fibre is important as it prevents constipation and increases the speed with which food passes through the gut. Wholemeal bread and flour, brown sugar, brown rice, pulses, vegetables (especially the skins) and fruit are all good sources of fibre.

The following menu suggests a healthy diet for one day. The lunch and supper can be reversed.

Sample diet

Breakfast	○ Wheat cereals, such as Weetabix, with whole milk, or toast (wholemeal) with peanut butter or marmite.
Lunch	○ Wholemeal bread sandwiches with cheese and tomato, egg, peanut butter, or marmite and lettuce. ○ Fruit or yoghurt.
Snack	○ Wholemeal biscuits or fruit.
Supper	○ Meat, fish or beans with potatoes, carrots and peas. ○ Rice pudding or stewed apple and ice cream.
Drinks	○ Milk, apple or orange juice, tea, unsweetened squash.

Although it is not a good idea to let your child eat snacks and sweets regularly, an occasional treat, such as an ice-cream, will not do him any harm.

A child will feel a sense of achievement when he is able to help himself at the table.

Snacks between meals

Eating between meals is a constant source of irritation to many parents. Particularly in the preschool age group, young children often seem to have an enormous appetite, which needs to be satisfied with between-meal snacks. This is not usually due to greediness, because children of this age have a genuine need for large amounts of food to build their fast-growing frames. All you have to do is to make sure that these snacks are properly nutritious. This means that you should not take the easy route of giving your child unlimited amounts of 'junk food' like crisps and sweets just to shut him up and stop him worrying you. Give him snacks like cheese and fruit instead. They will fill him up, and they won't cause overweight or health problems later.

In a few cases, a child may be genuinely greedy, and if he is putting on too much weight, you may need to cut down on the between-meal snacks, or at least make sure that they are not packed with sugar. Similarly, your child has to accept that snacks are not a substitute for proper meals. Some children are so involved in their play that they resent the need to take breaks to eat their meals, and are happy to wander around eating snacks so they can continue with their own activities. This sort of eating should be firmly discouraged, because eventually you will lose control of his diet, and he will subsist entirely on convenience foods which may not be at all good for him in the long term.

Another problem with too much eating between meals is that a child may consume so much that he doesn't want anything to eat when he is sat at the table for mealtime. Lack of appetite can also be caused by giving a child too much fruit juice or milk between meals. As with snacks, moderation is best.

Don't be too dogmatic about *not* eating between meals, because there will always be exceptions to the rule. If you are out shopping with your child, for example, you may not be able to provide him with a 'proper' meal at the right time, and here a snack could be useful.

If a child is a fussy eater, helping with cooking may well stimulate an interest in food.

Care of the Teeth

By the time he is $2\frac{1}{2}$, your child should have his full set of milk teeth, with a total of ten teeth in each jaw. The first teeth to come through the gum are at the front, but as the larger molar teeth at the back of the jaw come through the gum, these can be very uncomfortable.

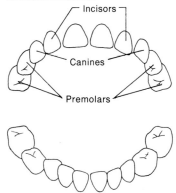

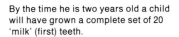

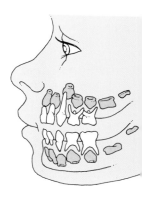

By the time he is two years old a child will have grown a complete set of 20 'milk' (first) teeth.

At about six years the permanent adult teeth begin to erupt through the jaw behind the milk teeth.

It's never too early to take care of the teeth. You should train your child to clean his teeth as early as possible – but you will still have to check that he has cleaned them properly for several years to come. The most important factors to remember are to get him a proper child's toothbrush, with a small enough head to get properly to the back of his mouth, and to train him to clean the teeth with an up-and-down movement which will dislodge food particles and plaque from the gaps between the teeth, and the back of the teeth.

It is important that a child learns to clean his teeth with an up-and-down movement rather than a side-to-side motion.

Most children regard cleaning the teeth as a rather boring adult game, which they enliven by eating the toothpaste. This is not a good idea, so try to get fluoride toothpaste which is not strongly flavoured, and especially, is not one of the fruit-flavoured junior types, which will certainly be eaten. Many children as well as adults find it easiest to scrub the toothbrush across the teeth from side to side. This is bad practice, because it scores the teeth and the scratches form a focus for later decay. Stick to the up-and-down movements which allow the bristles to penetrate into the gaps between the teeth, and if you can afford it, consider buying a battery-powered toothbrush, which children love and which actually clean the teeth very efficiently.

As your child gets a little older, he can be shown the importance of cleaning his teeth properly by introducing him to disclosing tablets. You can buy these cheaply at the chemist, and when they are chewed, they will stain plaque remaining around the teeth after cleaning, so it can be clearly seen. The first time your child sees a spectacular red stain around his teeth, he will appreciate the need for proper cleaning!

Most toothpaste contains fluoride nowadays, and this has led to a great improvement in the health of children's teeth, with cavities becoming much less common. It is tempting for parents to check their child's teeth, and because they think they cannot see any sign of damage, to put off a proper dental checkup. This attitude is probably influenced by the fear many adults have of going to the dentist.

Getting him used to the dentist

It's never too early to get your child's teeth looked at by the dentist, once the first teeth have appeared. There may be obvious cavities, or there could be hair-fine cracks which could lead to decay if they are not treated properly.

More important, the dentist can give you advice on keeping your child's teeth healthy. It is not sufficient to use fluoride toothpaste. In most areas, your child will need extra fluoride to protect his teeth, and the dentist will be able to advise you on the best way to do this, and on the right amount of fluoride to give (usually as drops or tablets).

It won't take your child too long to realize that on most of his visits to the dentist, nothing painful happens, so there is really no reason to be frightened. It's worth checking with friends and acquaintances to see if they use a dentist who is good with children, because at this age, they can easily be frightened by someone with a brusque manner. In most areas, there will be a dental clinic specializing in the care of children's teeth, and this is a logical place to start.

In the dental surgery or clinic there will be leaflets and other publications which will give detailed advice on the care of your child's teeth, and the dentist will be able to give any additional

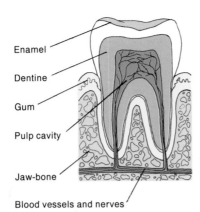

Enamel

Dentine

Gum

Pulp cavity

Jaw-bone

Blood vessels and nerves

In a healthy tooth the pulp cavity, which contains the blood vessels and nerves, is protected by a layer of dentine and a layer of hard enamel. However, if the teeth aren't cleaned properly bacteria in the mouth convert sugars from food into acid. The acid eats into the enamel and dentine, eventually allowing bacteria to infect the pulp cavity and thereby cause toothache.

advice you may need. Never be afraid to ask lots of questions. After all, you are helping to preserve the health of your child's teeth for the rest of his life. In particular, the dentist will make sure that your child knows how to brush his teeth thoroughly, and can supply or recommend the proper type of brush and toothpaste.

Another important aspect of a dental checkup is that the dentist will be able to check that the milk teeth are coming through in the proper place. It is common for the first teeth to be slightly misplaced in the jaw, and this will lead to problems later when the adult teeth come through, and there may not be sufficient space for them on the jaw. Some minor orthodontic treatment now can make sure that the later adult teeth will be attractive and even.

Fear of the dentist

Sooner or later, most children need a filling, and however skilful your dentist may be, it's always going to be an uncomfortable experience for a child. So there is no point in brushing aside your child's fears and telling him that it won't hurt. It's far better to be honest, and tell him that it will be a bit uncomfortable for a little while, but that afterwards everything will be fine – and that if he didn't have the filling, it would soon be *really* painful. You will need to explain to him, in simple terms, exactly what is wrong with his tooth, and what the dentist is going to do. Don't make too much of a production of this, or he will be deeply suspicious about the whole procedure. Often the dentist will spend some time showing him the drill and other gadgets, so he can see what is producing the loud noise in his mouth.

If your child is really frightened of dental work, it can make the dentists job very difficult. He cannot undertake dental treatment on a frightened and unwilling child, so you need to discuss with the dentist, *away from your child*, the best way to proceed. In view of the importance of dental health, he may recommend that the

○ Disclosing tablets can help teach children the importance of proper oral hygiene by revealing plaque remaining on the teeth after cleaning.

work be carried out later, under a light anaesthetic. This needs your careful consideration, and is probably best carried out in a large dental clinic, where a qualified anaesthetist is available.

For most routine examinations and procedures, your child won't be frightened at all. After his first few visits to the dentist he finds out that there is nothing to be worried about, and it becomes just another part of his routine. And of course he is reassured by your own regular visits to the dentist, where he can see that you are not worried about it. You do go for regular checkups, don't you? Remember that as in most other things, children learn from your example.

Keeping Clean – Washing and Hygiene

By age three, a daily bath is usually fun, or it may be a boring interruption into play. Preschool children seldom understand the *need* for a bath or wash, and most are not too disturbed by a little dirt or by feeling sweaty in hot weather. There is no point in trying to explain the need for hygiene to them, because they have no concept of bacteria or disease. You have instead to make sure that regular and thorough washing becomes a habit which fits automatically into the daily routine.

Bathtime

Children of all ages enjoy playing in the bath, although by five or six years they may feel they are too important to admit to such childish pursuits. So let them have as many toys in the bath as they wish, and let them splash about. There is no way in which you can expect children of three to six years to bath without flooding the whole room, so you must resign yourself to clearing up after them.

You will certainly have to wash younger children yourself. Face washing is always a problem, because it can be uncomfortable, and no one likes to get soap in their eyes. You must always be careful and gentle when washing your child's face, or you can expect tears and tantrums. In fact, your washing of his face is a powerful incentive for a child to learn to wash himself, so he can take control of the flannel. But you must still supervise, and give a final check around the neck and behind the ears.

The use of special children's bubble bath is sensible, because it cleanses the child as he plays, and the foam is less uncomfortable than soap if it gets in his eyes.

A few children are still nervous about water even at age three, and you can increase their confidence by letting them use the shower attachment to wash off the bubbles from a foam bath. Encourage this by putting in lots of bubble bath, so it's difficult to get the bubbles off any other way.

Showers

Showering is a perfectly good alternative to a bath, and is much less time consuming. Your child gets just as clean, though you may get wetter. If you don't have a shower, fit a temporary shower attachment to the bath taps. It will be useful for washing and rinsing the hair.

Supervision

However much fun bathtime may be, it is potentially hazardous. Any child can slip and hit his head, and could drown in only a few inches of water. Toddlers love playing with taps, and could turn on the hot water and scald themselves seriously if not supervised. The moral is obvious. Don't take chances with your child's life, and keep a close eye on them in the bath. *Never leave them alone.*

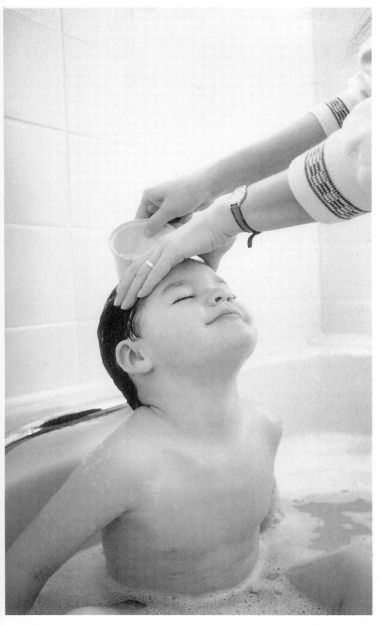

○ Washing a child's hair is perhaps most easily combined with his normal bathtime.

This applies even more when you bath two children together. Slippery children can easily fall and bang their heads, and when one child is older than the other, accidentally-on-purpose pushes can be expected. Horseplay in the bath is definitely not to be encouraged.

The real answer to supervision in the bath is your own common sense. Obviously most five-year-olds can be trusted to bath themselves safely (but not necessarily thoroughly), so they will need less supervision than a three-year-old. But it would not be sensible to let them lock the door to ensure their own privacy, despite the 'modesty' which young children often affect around age five or six.

Washing hands and face should be routine after every meal and at bedtime.

By the time she starts school, she should be able to wash and dry herself.

Face and hands

It won't do any harm to miss out the occasional bath if you have been out for the day, and bedtime is approaching. But you must make very sure that face and hands are washed regularly, preferably before *and* after meals, for reasons of hygiene (and because it's not pleasant to eat alongside a grubby toddler).

Hand washing after using the toilet is absolutely essential. This means proper scrubbing with soap, not just a cursory rinse under the tap. (See also 'Care of the nails', p.59.)

Personal Care

There are several ways in which a toddler can begin to learn self-care, and these will eventually lead to him becoming aware of his own appearance and image. Once he realizes that it's not just his parents, but also his friends who expect him to meet certain standards of appearance and cleanliness, he will gradually become motivated to care for himself. Don't despair if your child seems not to have the slightest interest in his appearance – some children seem to take many years to get the idea.

Looking after the hair

Very young children *hate* having their hair washed. They don't like getting shampoo in their eyes (even though you should be using the non-stinging type), they don't like lying down or leaning forward for their hair to be wet, they don't like having their hair towelled dry, and they don't like having the tangles combed out either.

So how can you make hair care more acceptable? Probably the easiest answer is to keep the whole process as brief as possible, and just get on with it regardless of the screams! It is socially acceptable for boys to have short hair and they can be introduced to the hairdresser at an early age. They usually appreciate the comfort of short hair, and the fact that it can be dried very quickly after washing.

For little girls, care of the hair is a more serious business. As soon as they realize that girls are actually different from boys, they become aware that many other small girls have long hair, and they usually want to copy them. If they *want* long hair, they usually accept the need for more complicated hair washing, and also understand that their hair needs to be brushed thoroughly if it is to look nice afterwards. Girls (and many boys) often enjoy fussing with the hair dryer, though they need to be supervised in case they burn themselves or use the dryer for too long.

Many small girls don't like having their hair messed about, and would rather concentrate on the rough and tumble of toddler play than have their hair washed and brushed. If your little girl is not interested in the appearance of her hair, don't keep her hair long just because you think it looks pretty. Let her be comfortable and happy, and wait until she shows more interest in hair care before you encourage her to grow it longer. You can always show her how hair can be plaited to keep it out of the way and tidy while she is playing.

It is important that a young child has his own hair brush and comb, and is shown how to use them properly. You will have used a very soft hair brush at first, for fear of hurting him, but once he can brush his own hair, get one with stiffer bristles which do a better job of removing tangles. He won't use it roughly enough to hurt himself. When you buy a comb, check that it does not have sharp teeth which could scratch the scalp.

○ Long hair may be attractive, but it needs extra care and attention in order to keep it looking tidy.

How often should you wash the hair? It can be as often as you like but should be at least twice a week. If your child has very long hair which takes a long time to dry, it may be too time-consuming to wash it daily. It is often easiest to combine hair washing with bathtime or a shower, when your child is already thoroughly wet.

If tangles cause tears when brushing or combing the hair, use a conditioner, which helps to lubricate the hair so the brush or comb slips through more easily. You may need to experiment until you find one which does the job best.

For older children, it is sometimes possible to wash the hair at the sink. To do this, you will have to sit the child with his head tipped back over the sink, pouring warm water over his hair from a jug. It seems hardly worth the trouble though, because a wriggling toddler will usually manage to soak himself and you, so it would have been quicker to have dumped him in the bath for hair washing.

Lice and nits

When you are brushing his hair, look very carefully for lice and nits. These small parasites are quite common in toddlers once they start playing with other children, and are spread by contact. Contrary to popular belief, lice and nits have nothing to do with being dirty or unhygienic – in fact, they are most common in long, well-groomed hair. Signs of lice include an itchy scalp due to bites (particularly when the child is hot) and the presence of tiny, greyish-white eggs (known as nits). These are found close to the scalp and are difficult to remove. If you see any signs of nits, or if the clinic or nurse finds them, don't feel insulted. Just ask the pharmacist for the appropriate type of medicated shampoo and follow the instructions for use. This will kill the lice and you can simply remove the dead nits with a fine comb. All members of the family should be treated with the shampoo as a precaution.

Use a small pair of nail scissors to keep your child's nails short and smooth, following the shape of the finger or toe.

Care of the nails

Care of the nails is, together with hand washing, an important factor in hand hygiene. You will have to show your child how to use a nail brush to clean properly under the nails. Unlike other forms of washing, dirt under the nails is very obvious, so he can see what he is supposed to scrub clean. Use a proper nail brush and soap to make sure that all the dirt is removed.

It is important to keep the nails short, so it is easy to keep them clean and so that he does not scratch himself or other people. Use small curved nail scissors and trim the nail so it is level with the finger tip, or a little shorter than this. Trim them evenly, following the curve of the finger or toe. If your child makes a fuss about having his nails cut, try using clippers. It is another essential routine and so despite the tantrums you must continue to cut his nails. Some children get distressed and want them "put back". Explain what you are doing and why.

Clothes and Dressing

Up until age three, you have probably dressed your child primarily for comfort and convenience, except for special occasions. Easily washed and durable clothes like denim are most practical for small children, who don't usually express any particular dress preferences, except for liking bright colours and enjoying 'dressing up' games.

○ Like dressing up, face-painting can be great fun.

○ Choosing new clothes is often a compromise between practicality and the child's own taste.

Practical choices

As your child becomes older, he will become aware of clothes, and the differences between them. In particular, he will notice what other children wear, and may want to copy them. Unfortunately, it will be several years before your child can appreciate the differences between clothes which are for playing in, and the expensive clothes which are to be kept for special occasions. He will not understand that the clothes you dressed him in to go to a party are not suitable for tree-climbing or digging up the garden, and the only way he can learn is the expensive way – while you clean up or repair the damage.

Outdoor clothes need to be tough enough to withstand the rough and tumble of play in all weathers.

The only remedy is to maintain the distinction between everyday clothes and 'special' clothes. Making it clear that certain clothes are only to be worn under special circumstances *may* encourage your child to take more care of them – until he forgets, during all the excitement. Expensive, dry clean only clothes just aren't practical for the average child.

For all normal wear, the standard child's uniform of jeans or shorts worn with T-shirt, sweater or anorak is both practical and economical. That way, your child will feel free to play without restrictions, and you will not have to worry too much about damage to valuable clothes. For certain activities, such as painting or cooking, a pinafore or apron is still useful, and will keep a certain amount of mess off his clothes. Long-sleeved, plastic aprons are the most useful. However, don't forget that if it's hot dressing your child in very few clothes will reduce your washing load still more.

Making dressing easier
Look for clothes which are easy to put on, with simple but robust fastenings, and avoid heavy clothes which restrict movement, and will be hated by an active child.

You should make every effort to encourage your child to dress himself at an early age. Most children can quickly cope with zip fasteners, but will probably not be able to engage the bottom of the zip in an anorak without help for several years. Buttons can be difficult for small fingers, especially small buttons in new clothes, where the fabric is still stiff and some degree of strength and dexterity is needed to do them up.

Similarly, buckles on shoes are large and are generally easy for a child to do up, while tying laces can be very difficult. Few children can tie a bow in shoelaces until age five, and many cannot manage even then. This is a particular problem for left-handed children, whose coordination is not quite so good as right-handed children, and who find it difficult to reverse a 'normal' knot by copying a right-handed adult. You can get round this problem by buying him shoes which slip on or buckle or have Velcro fastenings, and will be easier to secure.

Because young children have little sense of appropriate dress, you may have problems when they insist on wearing their favourite clothes or shoes. They may want to wear winter boots on a hot day, or decide that a T-shirt is appropriate wear for a winter's day. This can cause tearful scenes, and you may have to explain tactfully to your child why you don't think that his choice of clothes is right for a particular occasion, or if it is not too outrageous give in and let him find out for himself.

○ Zips and other fasteners can be fiddly for small fingers.

Using the Toilet

By the age of three, most children are able to control their urine and bowel movements reliably during the day, and can usually use the pot without supervision. You may also have converted them to use of the normal toilet, by using a training seat which fits over the pan, but this can sometimes cause difficulties.

Full-size toilets

It's hardly surprising that small children find that using an adult toilet can be a bit worrying after the comfortable plastic pot they have been used to. After all, how would you feel about using a toilet that was very nearly as tall as you, and large enough to drown in?

You should make use of the toilet as simple as possible for your child. Give him a small stool or box to climb up on, and fit a plastic training seat so he feels secure and knows he can't fall in! Many children still feel very insecure on a full-size toilet for a while, and this shows up as constipation, when they defer bowel movements for as long as possible. It is a good idea to keep the old familiar pot handy for a while, so he knows he can use it whenever he wants.

Keeping dry

Once you have accustomed your child to using your own toilet, you should not expect him to be fully confident when he uses other toilets. He will need time to get used to the idea of using a strange toilet, and may therefore put off going for so long that an 'accident' happens. Children are especially wary of using public toilets, because they are not accustomed to carrying out 'private' toilet functions in noisy circumstances with large numbers of people about. Small boys are often very anxious about using urinals in public toilets, and may be upset at seeing unfamiliar adults exposing themselves while urinating. There are also obvious reasons why it is unwise to allow small boys to use public toilets unescorted by another adult.

At first, both boys and girls urinate in a sitting position, with the pants pulled down or removed. Boys sometimes find it difficult to make the transition to urinating while standing up, because there are several problems for them to overcome:

○ They need to open their trousers and fiddle with their pants before they can urinate. It's much easier if they have trousers with elasticated waists.

○ The toilet is usually much to high for them to reach, unless they have a box or stool handy. This can cause problems in using the toilet in other people's houses.

○ Expect accidents, because their aim is poor!

A step will help a small boy when using a full-size toilet.

Obviously girls will not experience these problems, but you can expect a few difficulties once girls realize that it is possible to urinate while standing up, and they try to experiment.

Coping with 'accidents'

Up to age six, and even after, it is not uncommon for a child to have an 'accident'. The bladder capacity of a child is quite small, especially in boys, so they need to urinate quite frequently.

Involuntary urination can be caused by stress, excitement or anxiety, as well as by a full bladder, and when a child wants to urinate in a strange environment but is frightened to ask to use the toilet, accidents are common. Similarly, if he is engrossed in a fascinating game and defers urinating for as long as possible, or ignores the warning signs of an over-full bladder, an 'accident' is very likely.

Some children dribble urine continually, and more especially when they are overexcited or tired. There is sometimes a physical reason for this, and you should discuss the problem with the doctor, but *not* in the child's hearing, or you will make him even more anxious.

Because parents are now advised never to pressure their child into toilet training, there is sometimes the possibility that by leaving him in nappies they are making things just too easy for him, so he never bothers to go to the trouble of learning to control his bladder. While no enlightened modern parent would want to worry their child by making too much fuss about being dry, it is sensible to make sure that your child knows you would like him to be dry. If you don't mind clearing up after a few accidents, wearing ordinary pants or training pants may make it more obvious to him that being wet is uncomfortable, and give him the incentive to learn to control his bladder more effectively.

Bowel control

Parents are much more anxious about bowel movements than their children. This is because most adults have been brought up to believe that they should move their bowels every day. But children do not think in this way, and they do not time their bowel movements either. Some children pass stool only every two to three days, and this is perfectly normal. Others may go two or three times each day, and this is equally normal. In practice most children and adults tend to pass stool after a meal, and many parents use this fact to advantage in toilet training.

Despite the best efforts of their parents, almost all children soon decide that there is something dirty about passing stools (probably because of talking to other children), and they usually prefer to use the toilet in private. Despite this, most children need help in wiping their bottoms, even up to age five or six. You will need to teach them how to cope with this essential function competently before they go to school, as they will otherwise become extremely shy about the whole thing, and try to defer using the toilet until they get home.

You will have to teach your child how to wipe his bottom thoroughly, and in the case of girls, to wipe from the front towards the back, so they don't smear faeces onto the vagina.

Make sure that thorough hand washing with soap and water becomes an automatic sequel to moving the bowels.

Getting caught short

While your child is very small, you can carry a pot with you when you go out shopping or on family outings. This is not so easy when he is a bit older, and doesn't want to use the pot any more. Some children become so used to using the toilet that they feel inhibited about urinating out in the open, if they cannot find a suitable toilet. Other children may be completely unconcerned about urinating in public. A shy child may need to be reassured that there is nothing wrong or dirty about relieving themselves in this way, but that it is only to be done in an emergency.

Sexual hygiene

Some parents become very concerned about 'sexual hygiene', imagining all sorts of unpleasant conditions which could affect the sex organs of their child unless they are constantly cared for and washed thoroughly. In fact, the reverse is true. Provided the sex organs have developed properly (and the doctor and health visitor will have checked this thoroughly) it is unlikely that any real problems will occur in young children.

The sex organs are largely self-cleaning, and do not need special attention other than normal bathing and washing. In particular, you should never attempt to wash inside the vagina of a little girl, as this could introduce infection. Occasionally, a vaginal discharge may appear in girls, but this should be reported to the doctor for proper treatment rather than attempting to 'wash it away'.

Some people believe that in uncircumcised boys, the foreskin should be pulled back so the tip of the penis can be washed properly. This is completely unnecessary, unless it has been specifically recommended by the doctor for medical reasons, usually because of recurring infections.

Fear of a 'tight foreskin' is largely myth, and attempting to roll back the foreskin can be harmful because it may cause small tears and scars which could become infected. If there is any problem, the doctor may recommend circumcision. This minor operation to remove the foreskin is sometimes carried out shortly after birth, for religious or social reasons, but is seldom necessary for medical reasons.

○ Toilet hygiene should be learnt before starting school.

SEXUALITY

The Beginnings of Sexuality

Many parents dread the day that their child will start to ask embarrassing questions about her body and where she came from. They don't want to stimulate an 'unhealthy' interest in sex, but neither do they want to avoid the issue. And worst of all, many adults just feel uncomfortable about the idea of talking about sex to their child.

Some form of discussion about sex cannot be avoided for ever. At some time, the child will notice that her own body looks different from pictures she sees in a book or on the television. She will probably be confused and worried, because she cannot associate her own small, smooth body with the large and hairy bodies of adults. Her first signs of interest in other people's bodies usually follow seeing a naked child of the opposite sex, with whom she can associate more closely than an adult. She will inevitably want to know why a little boy has a penis and she does not. And she will want to know what the sex organs are called.

The only sensible response to these perfectly natural enquiries is to answer them, without fuss and without launching into a long and complicated lecture on sex. This would only baffle her, because at this stage, she is no more interested in sex than in anything else she encounters, so she would not understand the reason for your long-winded response to her simple question.

The age at which this sort of interest arises varies, but most children are curious about the differences between boys and girls around age three or four. When feeling anxious, a four-year-old will often grasp the genitals as a form of comfort, and children of this age also handle their genitals when they feel the need to urinate. At age five, most children begin to show signs of self-consciousness about their bodies, and from then on, begin to develop real sexual curiosity, discussing sex with their friends, and often exploring each other's bodies.

"Where did I come from?"

This is one of the earliest, and the most important questions a child will ask about sex. As with other sexual matters, don't confuse the first casual question with a need for a detailed lecture on sexual anatomy and obstetrics. In fact, all she probably wants is to be told that she grew "in Mummy's tummy". Other questions such as "How did I get out?" and "How did Daddy put me there?" will follow, and should be answered simply.

If you try to avoid embarrassing yourself by telling her 'harmless' fairy stories about the stork or being left under a gooseberry bush, you will only put off the day when she talks to other children about sex, and it dawns on her that her parents have not been honest.

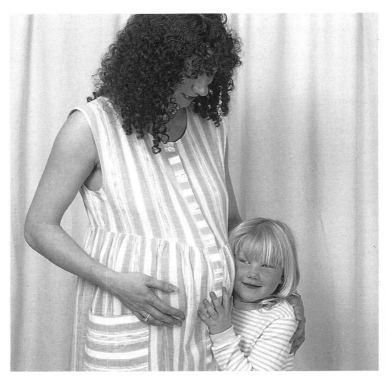

○ Sex education can be introduced when a new baby is expected.

The easiest and most natural time to introduce the subject of babies and where they come from is when you (or a close family friend) are expecting another child. In this way, she can be told what is happening, and how the baby was produced, and can see the reality of the event as the swelling in your stomach develops.

Don't worry about frightening a child with the details of lovemaking. It will be several years before she makes the association between what you have been telling her and the structure of her own small body. Small girls usually accept the future reality of a baby growing inside their own body, and are therefore quite unconcerned about the whole thing.

Understanding appropriate behaviour
It is difficult to explain to a young child what sort of sexual behaviour is appropriate, partly because different families have their own codes of conduct in these matter. For example, some people are very relaxed about nudity, while others preserve their modesty at all times. What you will need to do is to explain to your child what is acceptable to you, and to your immediate circle of family and friends. This needs to be handled sensitively, because you don't want her to feel that everything to do with her

body and about sex is 'dirty' and is never to be discussed. On the other hand, sooner or later you will want her to appreciate that, when you have visitors, the toilet door should be closed when she defecates, or that you may not want a naked six-year-old wandering through the lounge if you have guests.

It can be difficult to decide what you consider to be 'acceptable behaviour' when you find your child playing with another, and exploring each other's bodies. What you may dismiss as harmless play in three-year-olds may be more disturbing in six-year-olds. In practice, the undeveloped nature of their bodies means that in neither case will they come to any physical ill-effects, although in the case of the older children, it is wise to explain very firmly that this is *not* acceptable behaviour, now that they are growing up. These fumbling attempts at sexuality sometimes lead to objects being experimentally pushed into the vagina; a practice which can lead to dangerous infection and must be stopped immediately.

Masturbation

It can be very disturbing and embarrassing for parents (and even more so for grandparents) when they see a young child masturbating. This is usually because adults find it difficult or uncomfortable to believe that a young child can have 'adult' sexual feelings.

Although masturbation may seem 'wrong', there is little direct sexual element in this activity, at least in the early years. Most children below one-year-old play with their genitals, as part of their self-exploration. In a few children, the habit becomes compulsive, and as they grow older and begin to understand their social surroundings, it may be necessary to explain to them that, although there is nothing wrong with the habit, it should not be done in public. You should avoid raising feelings of guilt and anxiety by telling them that this is wrong, as the habit is harmless. Habitual masturbation in children is usually a comfort habit, rather like sucking the thumb. Masturbation is much more common in boys than in girls.

Nudity

Nudity is a subject that arouses strong feelings in many families, despite the almost commonplace topless (and bottomless) bathing that takes place on most holiday beaches, and the regular displays of nudity in newspapers and on television. Children are usually quite familiar with the appearance of the nude adult body, however their parents choose to treat the subject.

Some families adopt the traditional attitude of hiding their bodies modestly behind towels, or turning their backs while dressing. Others make a point of walking about naked in front of their children. In each case, the parents are trying to make a point, showing that they are much more worried about nudity than their children. Small children show little interest in the naked body, after having had a look and asked "What's that?" a few times, until their curiosity is satisfied. The most sensible option is to relax about nudity, not snatching up a towel if your child walks into the bathroom, thus making her curious, but equally not making a point of flaunting yourself in front of her.

If your child senses that nudity is a subject which bothers you she is likely to make a point of shocking you by trying to catch you naked, or by parading around naked herself at an embarrassing moment, such as when you have visitors.

Sharing the bath with a parent is enjoyed by most children and in this way their curiosity is satisfied at an early age. You may still be bombarded with mildly embarrassing questions about adult sex organs, but it will be a long while before a small boy makes the association between his own tiny sex organs and those of his father, or a girl realizes that a baby could be produced from her own vagina.

Lack of inhibitions

Even though some children may be uneasy at the sight of naked adults, few have any inhibitions about their own body, and in warm weather, play happily with little or nothing on. Provided you are confident that she won't produce an unexpected puddle or worse, there can be no objections to her running about naked indoors or out. What you have to decide is the age at which this is no longer automatically socially acceptable, and this can be difficult. Some older people "Tut, tut" with disapproval at the very thought of a baby playing naked on the beach, let alone a toddler. Yet it seems silly to put a small child into a bathing costume to play, and still more silly to see a little girl wearing a two-piece bikini to preserve her non-existent modesty. And what is perfectly acceptable on a holiday beach may be definitely out of order in your local park. So be sensitive to other people's attitudes towards nudity, especially with older pre-school children.

Awkwardness about nudity usually only comes when your child starts to mix with others, and enjoys 'naughty' conversations with her friends. When this happens, you will probably notice a sudden change in her attitude towards your body, as well as her own. She may show signs of interest where before she was indifferent, or shyness when before she was casual about nudity. If this happens, you must be careful not to change your own habits to conform to her new attitude. If you do, you will confirm to her that you were kidding her along all the time, and were not just being natural.

Sexual abuse

Sexual abuse is sadly on the increase, and children of all ages are susceptible regardless of social class. Abuse can take place at the hands of an adult, but more frequently is caused by an older child, who is often a brother or sometimes a sister. Serious sexual abuse resulting in rape of a small boy or girl is usually immediately apparent to the parent, because considerable physical damage and pain results. Other forms of abuse are less obvious, and can usually only be detected by a sudden change in behaviour in the abused child. For example, a child who has previously had only normal passing interest in sexual matters may start to talk incessantly about sex, or may show precocious sexual behaviour such as becoming over-affectionate towards her father, or in the case of a boy, putting his hand up his mother's dress. Other children become very withdrawn and uncommunicative, or may revert to bed-wetting.

A change in behaviour of this type is usually completely innocent, and is probably caused by other factors. However, parents should be alert to the possiblities of abuse and should consider what might have happened to cause the change in behaviour (or may be continuing to happen). If you have such suspicions, you have a difficult decision to make. If you press your child to tell you about it, and she has not been abused, she will be totally confused at your questioning, and will become very anxious. On the other hand, if abuse has taken place, she may become very distressed. Gentle questioning may give you the answer you need.

If you can confirm that abuse has taken place, you must consider if you can put a complete stop to it yourself (as is usually the case when another child is involved), or if you need to involve other people. The legal and social implications are potentially very serious, and your first step should be to seek expert advice from someone you can trust.

Possible signs of sexual abuse

○ **Physical signs of sexual abuse** Your child may complain of being sore in the genital area, or you may notice discharge, bleeding, cuts or bruising around the genitals.

○ **Signs of physical abuse** You may see bruises or hand imprints on your child's body, or she may suffer unexplained fractures.

○ **Behavioural changes** Your child may become sexually aware, behaving in a sexually precocious manner, constantly talking about sex, and masturbating. She may start behaving uncharacteristically, for example becoming secretive, running away from home or being difficult to manage.

○ **Third party** A friend, relative or neighbour may tell you they suspect someone is abusing your child.

Pink for a Boy? – Sexual Stereotypes

Nowadays it is unfashionable to force a sexual identity on a child. It is not thought appropriate to insist that boys will always be given certain types of 'masculine' toys, and encouraged to play robust games, while girls are given 'feminine' toys, and discouraged from rough and unladylike play. This is because it is now recognized that the distinction between the sexes, in terms of their behaviour, is not as strongly marked as had been previously assumed. Many psychologists believe that 'male' and 'female' behaviour is largely learned from family and society, and that if children were left to select their own preferences, these differences would be much less marked.

Inherent differences or social conditioning?

Boys always seem to be more interested in playing with mechanical toys like cars than girls, while girls tend to be interested in toys which mimic domestic activities. This is partly because children tend to copy a role model of the same sex. So boys will play at activities which resemble their father's interests, while girls model themselves on their mothers. In families where the parents split their roles so that they both take part in household chores and childcare, this tendency to stereotyped sexual behaviour will probably not be so apparent. Books and television can also effect a child's views.

In practice, however, there *is* an inbuilt difference in behaviour between boys and girls that seems to be independent of learned behaviour. These differences surface both in the sort of games children play and in the way that they play. Studies have shown that girls tend to play together in pairs, while boys prefer

Boys like to play in large groups and often favour noisy games that involve running around.

Sexual stereotyping extends even to the dressing-up clothes we give our children. In the past little girls were only given nurses' outfits to play in, now they are also encouraged to play doctors.

to play alone or in larger groups. Girls are also more likely to choose quieter games, such as dressing up or drawing, and have been shown to be more cooperative in play, especially when playing with younger children. Boys certainly tend to be more physically active and aggressive than girls of a corresponding age, and this leads to their interest in guns and 'war games'.

Many parents who object to the level of violence and aggression in our society will not let their small boys play with guns, hoping that this will lessen their aggression later on. However, this attitude ignores the basic curiosity of a child. By denying him a toy in which he has expressed an interest, and which he sees all his friends playing with, it is perfectly natural for him to want the same toy for himself, and for him to make a serious issue about obtaining it. In fact you may be merely drawing his attention to guns, and making them seem more appealing than they really are, because they have become 'forbidden fruits'. It is very doubtful if a small child has the slightest idea of what a real gun is, and the damage it can do.

The question of sexual identity of children is an interesting one, because it worries parents far more than it does their children. Most parents are highly illogical about the question of sexual identity, and would not dream of dressing even a newborn boy in pink, let alone an older child. They are happy to dress a girl in trousers, and let her play with toy cars, but are horrified if their small boy dresses up in one of his sister's dresses, or wants to play with dolls (although they are usually quite happy to let him play with dolls, provided they are called 'Action Man' or something equally masculine). Therefore, it is acceptable for a small girl to behave as a 'tomboy', but not acceptable for a boy to behave in a 'girlish' manner. Once a child goes to play group or nursery school, this distinction is broken down to some extent, because all children are taught to take part in formerly feminine activities, such as cooking.

PROBLEMS

Bedtime and Sleep Problems

Up to age three or four, toddlers have almost limitless energy, and can keep going for longer than their parents can tolerate them. At this age, subterfuge often has to be used to get them to go to bed when it suits you, and they are quite likely to bounce out again at inconvenient times of the night or early morning.

If you are lucky, your child will settle down quickly and make little fuss about going to bed and staying there, but for a large proportion of children, bedtime is a period of constant battle with their parents. Just talk to fellow parents and you will find that nearly all of them have some horror to tell about sleep patterns. There are various possible reasons for this.

Why won't he sleep?

○ He is not tired yet, and you are putting him to bed merely so you can get some peace and quiet, or spend some time alone with your partner.

○ He has been playing a complex game in which he has become totally involved, and bedtime disrupts his play completely. It takes time for the excitement to die down.

○ Something interesting is going on (such as the arrival of visitors), and he doesn't want to miss out.

○ You have not noticed that as he gets older, he needs less sleep, so you are now trying to put him to bed too early.

○ His other brothers and sisters have not gone to bed yet, so why should he?

○ He is sometimes punished by being sent to bed early, and fears you may be punishing him now.

○ He is testing your authority by defying you on one of the main 'family rules'.

If you are one of the lucky parents who never have problems in persuading their child to go to bed at the proper time, you can congratulate yourself. If not, it may help to consider some of the following points.

The bedroom as 'home'

A child spends a very large part of his life in his bedroom, and he needs to feel that it is a welcoming and secure place, which is 'his'. If you are lucky enough to have sufficient space in your home to provide him with a room of his own, then he will already feel secure and comfortable there, surrounded with his own toys and belongings. He will become even more attached to it if his room can be personalized with some of his own paintings pinned up on the wall, and decorations in bright colours to suit his taste.

It hardly needs to be said that, if he is to enjoy his room and feel 'at home' there, he should not be punished by being sent to his room or sent to bed.

If he has to share a room with other children, or still has to sleep in your own room, you will have to encourage him to feel that his own part of the room is private to him, and is arranged to suit his own needs. This may cause problems with older brothers or sisters who often object to this territorial attitude, and will invade his space with their own play.

Part of his 'home' is his bed, which should be a full-sized bed, rather than a small and narrow junior bed which will be useless in a year or so. You may be tempted to buy bunk beds if you have other children, and your children will often demand these, because they look like fun. They save space, but they have some serious disadvantages as well.

Potential problems with bunk beds

○ There will always be arguments about who sleeps on top.

○ A sleeping child will inevitably be woken when the other child gets into bed.

○ Both children will keep each other awake by talking and playing.

○ Toys and objects fall onto the child sleeping beneath.

○ It is very difficult to nurse a sick child sleeping in the upper bed.

Make the bed and the bedroom as appealing as possible for a young child, using brightly coloured duvets or bed covers, books conveniently placed within reach, a toy box and a light which the child can reach.

If space is not too much of a problem, try to leave as much floor space as possible for playing. It will be much easier to clear up clutter from a relatively open space than from a room which is full of separate tables, stools and chairs.

Try to encourage his feeling that his room is private, allowing him to close the door when he is playing, and avoiding bursting in and interrupting him at play. He will probably resent visitors being shown his room, unless he takes them in there himself. Encourage him to use his bedroom as a playroom as much as possible, pointing out that unlike the lounge, his toys don't have to be cleared away as soon as it's mealtime, or when it's time for him to go to bed.

Even when a ladder is provided for use with a bunk bed most children prefer clambering up and down the sides of the bed.

Television and bedtime

Television is, for most families, the greatest obstacle to getting a child off to bed at the 'proper' time. Once absorbed in a programme, most children are highly resentful at being dragged away to go to bed. The problem is largely of the parents' own making. If you allow your child to sit in front of the television for hour after hour, taking charge of the channels and determining what everyone else has to watch, then of course he will object to being sent off to bed. It is better not to let the situation develop in this way, telling him when there is a programme that he may like, letting him watch it without interruption, and then firmly switching off or changing channels.

Quite often, the plea to "Just watch this to the end" is merely a ploy to avoid having to go to bed. You can check this and take the appropriate action by making sure that the television is tuned to some extremely uninteresting (to a child) programme, at around bedtime!

If your child suffers from disturbed sleep (see pp.81–3) it is always worth checking on what he has been viewing just before bedtime, and insisting on a change of television programmes if you think that is responsible.

Getting off to sleep

You can't really expect a bouncing three-year-old to suddenly switch off and go straight to sleep when you put him to bed. Neither will a six-year-old who is old enough to have some definite ideas of his own about bedtime. You will know from your

A hot milky drink may help a child relax at bedtime.

own experience that the more you try to go to sleep (such as when you know you have to get up early the next day), the more your mind buzzes and keeps you awake. Children are no different.

What is needed is to wind down in the evening, just as you do yourself. This means gradually stopping the boisterous games which can get a child overexcited, and relaxing with television or a story, together with a cuddle. A long warm bath is a great help to relaxation too, and this can be followed by a hot drink, so your child is sleepy and relaxed, all ready for bed.

Even though he seems tired, don't just switch off the light, but read to him or let him play for a while until he is really sleepy. Then give him his goodnight cuddle before tucking him down for the night. Don't worry if you hear him playing quietly or talking to himself for a while, because he will soon drop off to sleep. But if he climbs out of bed and starts banging about with some noisy game, you must explain to him quite firmly that this is not allowed.

A bedtime story can be an enjoyable routine for both parent and child.

Nightmares and night fears

All children experience nightmares at some time, and wake up screaming or crying. Sometimes these are true nightmares, occurring while in deep sleep, while other forms of frightening semi-dreams take place in the confused half-asleep time just before he drops off.

If you have a nightmare, you wake up feeling frightened and confused, but within a few moments, you regain your orientation and realize that it was only a dream. Children have much less of a grasp on reality than an adult, and find it difficult to separate the dream from real life, so they remain frightened for much longer after waking. Because they think that the nightmare was real, they are terrified of going back to sleep, in case it reappears. Unless they are quickly reassured they can become hysterical with fright.

Occasional nightmares affect almost all children and adults, but some children suffer from them regularly. These are usually sensitive children who are anxious or insecure in some way. They may have half-heard a conversation or argument that they continue to worry about until bedtime, and this leads to a nightmare. Things they have been told by other children, or have seen on the television can also prey on their minds and cause nightmares. Once the child has come to *expect* to suffer a nightmare, he will fear bedtime, become anxious and apprehensive, and almost guarantee himself another nightmare because of his fears. Nightmares are quite common if a child is feverish, or has a developing infection.

A related problem is night terrors; an unusual condition where you may find your child screaming with fear in the night, sitting up and apparently hallucinating, and not being conscious of your presence. A few children even get out of bed and run about while they are experiencing a night terror. These rare events are much more frightening for the parents than for the child, because he will probably not remember the incident in the morning. Usually it will end in the child suddenly relaxing and going off to sleep perfectly normally, leaving the parents quivering and upset.

With nightmares, night terrors, or any sleep disturbance which has frightened your child, reassurance is what he will need (see p.82).

Sleepwalking

Although sleepwalking is more common in children than in adults, it is rare in preschool children. If your child does sleepwalk talk to him in the day to try to discover if there is anything worrying him. To avoid accidents make sure that he cannot fall down the stairs, and tidy away toys that he might trip over. If you find him sleepwalking there is no need to wake him unless he is obviously having a nightmare or is disturbed. Instead simply guide him gently back to bed.

Coping with nightmares

○ Never, ever, leave him to cry. If your child wakes up screaming, you must get to him as fast as possible, so you can calm his fears before he gets too frightened.

○ Switch on the lights, so he can see that he is in his familiar bedroom.

○ Cuddle him, so he knows you are really there. His dream fears may have involved being left alone, or having lost his parents.

○ Keep talking, and keep reassuring him. Don't argue with him, and *never* tell him he is being silly, or try to laugh off his fears. You shouldn't worry about anything he says, even if it seems hurtful, because he is unlikely to know what he is saying, and it will probably still be part of his dream.

○ If he has left his bed, or wandered out of his room while sleepwalking, pick him up and put him back to bed without waking him. Waking up in an unexpected place would only frighten him more.

○ If he wakes up properly, give him a warm drink and a cuddle, and stay with him until he settles down again.

○ Consider giving him a dim nightlight, if this will reassure him.

Light sleepers

Despite all their parents' best efforts, some children just do not sleep very well. They may be difficult to settle down for the night, or they may wake up at the slightest disturbance. How you handle this depends to a large extent on how it affects your child. If he wakes up and plays quietly in bed, or looks at his books after putting on his light, you don't need to worry; he will sleep when he is tired enough, and won't suffer any after effects. Possibly you are putting him to bed too early, or he may be one of the many children who just don't seem to need much sleep.

However, if when he wakes he gets upset, or comes downstairs in the night, you need to consider why he does this, and how you should react. If a child is frightened of the dark, he will naturally be scared if he stirs in the night and finds everything in darkness. In this case, there are several nightlights which can be safely left on all through the night, using only small amounts of electricity. These provide sufficient light for the child to see that he is in familiar surroundings, but are not bright enough to glare and keep him awake.

He may wander downstairs an hour or so after bedtime, and this can be a difficult habit to break. It is probably due to the

○ Young children tire easily and on occasion may fall asleep at any time of the day.

feeling that he is missing out on whatever is going on, and if you scold him and bundle him back to bed, you will only reinforce this feeling. It's probably best to handle this situation by making sure that he doesn't find anything interesting happening, by ignoring him as far as possible, and carrying on with whatever you were doing. Once he understands that he will not get your attention, and that you definitely are not going to cooperate or play with him, he will probably wander off back to bed of his own accord. If you do cuddle him or let him begin to play, he will make sure that he comes down again on the next night, and you will simply be encouraging this habit.

For children who are genuinely light sleepers, and are woken by any noise, there is not much you can do except to try to make them as peaceful as possible. Discourage them from leaving their door open, and keep the television or stereo turned down a bit. Often this is only a passing phase, and their sleep is being affected by anxieties. You can't keep the whole house silent for them, and they will eventually learn to adjust to all the normal household noises and sleep more soundly.

Popping in every hour or so to make sure that a poor sleeper is alright is obviously not a good idea. Once the child realizes that this is a regular routine, he will lie there waiting for the next visit, so you will actually be keeping him awake.

How much rest?

The amount of sleep needed by a child varies with age, and between individual children. An infant sleeps nearly all the time, except when being fed, but needs progressively less sleep as he gets older. By age three, most children sleep for a total of about 12 hours each day, and part of this sleep period is in the form of an afternoon nap. After age four they probably will not sleep in the afternoon, and take all their rest at night. By age five, most children sleep for nine to ten hours each night, although some can make do with less. In practice, the occasional late night does no harm at all, and the child will make up for lost sleep over the next one or two nights.

What time to get up?

Young children tend to wake up when it becomes light, and this can be very irritating for their parents – especially on Sunday morning, when you probably want to lie-in. Blinds or thick curtains which darken the room may help your child to sleep a little later.

If your child always wakes early, you can try putting him to bed later, thus shifting his sleep patterns by an hour or so. Alternatively, give him lots of toys so he can play quietly in his bed when he wakes up. You will have to make it clear to him that you don't mind him playing quietly, but that he is not to disturb you until he hears you getting up, or until he hears your alarm clock going off.

It is also a good idea to try to give him a sense of time by putting a clock in his bedroom, and explaining to him that 'Getting-up time is when the big hand is on the twelve, and the little hand is on the seven'. You could perhaps mark these positions on the clock face with sticky tape, in case he doesn't understand properly.

Bed-wetting

Bed-wetting is a problem that is of great concern to most parents. It may not matter too much when your child is still in a cot, but once he has been transferred to an expensive 'grown-up' bed it can be very exasperating. His parents get cross when he wets the bed, he gets apprehensive and feels guilty, and the consequence is more wet beds.

The causes of the problem are actually very simple, but there is no simple cure. Bed-wetting is due to a combination of incomplete control over bladder function, and the small capacity of the bladder in a young child. He has not yet learned to respond to the normal signals which can wake up an adult in the middle of the night with the pressing need to urinate.

You will know when it's time to transfer your child to an adult bed when he wakes up dry more often than not. By this time, he will normally be capable of telling you when he needs the toilet during the daytime, or can go on his own. Don't tempt providence, but put a plastic cover over the mattress to protect it, and expect lots of accidents.

It is important that you do not react strongly in any way to a wet bed, avoiding praising him for being dry, and definitely not making a fuss when he is wet. All he needs is reassurance that as he is growing up, such accidents will become more and more rare. You can expect such accidents regularly until age five, and occasionally up to age seven or later.

Often a child who has been dry for a while will suddenly start to wet the bed again, and this is common between ages four to seven years. This is usually a short-term problem caused by some emotional upset, such as the arrival of a new baby, moving house, or going to a child minder or play group. As he gets used to the new situation, the bed-wetting problem usually clears up quickly.

Prolonged bed-wetting problems almost always clear up spontaneously as the child gets older. It seems to run in some families, and in general, boys are known to be more prone to bed-wetting than girls.

Dealing with bed-wetting

○ Provide a nightlight and make sure he has a pot to use, so he doesn't have to leave his room to go to the toilet.

○ If he seems to dribble urine continuously, consult the doctor, because he may have a physical problem.

○ If he seems to scratch his bottom or groin a lot, consult the doctor. The itching could be caused by worms, and he may urinate when the itching causes him to stir during the night.

○ Don't let him feel guilty about bed-wetting, even if grandparents or other people comment about it.

○ Cut down a bit on drinks in the evenings and at bedtimes, but not too much. If he goes to bed thirsty and thinking about a drink, he's quite likely to wet. On the other hand, don't encourage him to drink more than usual.

○ Try a battery-powered alarm if all else fails. This simple device is placed under the sheet, and 'beeps' as soon as it becomes damp. It can help to train him to wake at the warning signs of needing to urinate.

○ Consult the doctor if there is no sign of improvement after a few weeks, just in case there is some problem needing treatment.

The Overprotective Parent

The urge to protect your child is very strong, and is an important part of the family bond between parent and child. But it is easy to stray across the border between caring for your child, and being possessive and overprotective. Naturally you want to shield your child from harm. But you must remember that most of his learning comes from trial and error and example.

This means that you sometimes have to let your child learn by his mistakes. What it *doesn't* mean is allowing him to hurt himself or get into serious trouble, and you must be careful to supervise his experiments in independence. You can tell him constantly not to climb on the furniture in case he falls, but this will have almost no effect until he actually does fall, and sees that you were right after all. Similarly, telling your child that eating too many sweets will spoil his appetite is not a credible story – until he finds that he is too full up to enjoy his favourite meal.

Overprotecting a child means that the anxieties of the parents are reflected in the way they treat him, and this in turn affects his behaviour. A parent who is frightened of heights will make a great fuss about a small child climbing on a slide or a tree, and a non-swimming parent will be unhappy about their child playing in or near water. Even though they may not attempt to discourage their child from this type of activity, a child is sensitive enough to know that the parent is uneasy, so it will affect his behaviour indirectly. It is important to make a special effort to avoid transferring your own prejudices and fears to your child, in order that he can develop a personality of his own.

Being too overprotective is a form of repression. The over-protective parent is preventing the experimentation which leads to a bright and confident child, able to tackle any situation he encounters. Overprotected children are commonly shy, because their parents take the lead in every social encounter, and have made them feel inadequate.

Family factors

Only children, and the first children in a family are sometimes overprotected, because their parents can lavish all their love and care on them. But when another child comes along, the story is usually quite different, because attention has to be divided. So the eldest child may continue to be overprotected, because he now demands and accepts this, while the younger child or children are left more to their own devices. So the younger children are able to develop naturally, interacting well with other children, while the older child may become 'spoiled' and clingy.

Sometimes the youngest child in a large family is also overprotected, because the parents feel that this will be their last baby, and they want to make his childhood last as long as possible. It is not uncommon for the older children of the family to reinforce this attitude by also overprotecting the 'baby'.

Discipline – How Do You Cope?

Discipline means the development of a set of rules for life; at first just within the family, then for living in the community as a whole. Initially, discipline is imposed on a child by his parents and other members of the family, who lay down a code of acceptable behaviour to which they must adhere, and to which the child is also expected to conform. Later on, once the child understands and accepts these rules, they become a form of self-discipline, which he follows without question. They help him to learn to control his emotions and actions so that he becomes an acceptable member of the family and of society.

At first, you do most of his thinking for him, telling him what is right and what is wrong, and generally being there to monitor and referee his actions. As he gets older, he learns to take responsibility for his own actions, from deciding when to use the toilet, right up to decisions which could affect his safety, such as when to cross the road. As he gains greater understanding of the rules within which he must live, you gradually withdraw your own control to encourage his independence. Unfortunately, his wish to become independent often clashes with your own reluctance to withdraw control completely – a conflict which starts at preschool age and continues through adolescence.

Too much discipline is repressive, and crushes a child's spirit of adventure and independence. An over-disciplined child will be worried about trying anything new, and is often shy and clinging. After having been forced to comply with their parents' wishes at first, such children are liable to rebel against parental authority in later years, leading to a troubled adolescence.

Disciplining a child aged from three to six is not just a question of saying "No!", and setting out a list of rules which must not be broken. Discipline should be a much more positive approach, in which just as much is made of what he *can* do, or of what he is expected to do.

A visit to the supermarket can be a protracted battle of wills if a child persists in filling the trolley herself. Supermarkets that put sweets by the cash till cause extra problems.

As all parents know, children learn by example, and as the parents are the child's primary role models, he will be learning from their actions. If they are noisy and aggressive, then he will be the same. Equally, if the parents are inconsistent in their approach to discipline, tolerating some minor misbehaviour one day, then punishing him for it on another occasion, he will be confused and have little idea of right or wrong.

Discipline needs to be matched to the needs, age and temperament of the individual child. Obviously you should not expect a three-year-old to be as well-behaved at mealtimes as a six-year-old, because the younger child will not be so skilful with eating utensils, and will not understand the mealtime conventions you observe in your family. Similarly, some children have much more forceful and aggressive personalities than others, and will take longer to settle down to the sort of discipline you expect. Such children will probably never be as compliant as other, quieter children, so your expectations should be proportionately less, or else you will find yourself endlessly nagging and punishing them.

Practical rules for establishing discipline

○ Be honest; tell him why he may or may not do certain things, and be prepared to apologize if you are wrong yourself.

○ Be consistent, so he knows exactly what the rules are. If you and your partner disagree about discipline, don't argue about it in front of him – he will quickly learn to play one of you off against the other.

○ Reward good behaviour, but don't punish him for bad behaviour. He will soon realize that it's only the good behaviour that gets rewarded.

○ Be prepared to justify yourself. There is no point in telling him he must do something "Because I say so"; that way you lose all credibility and make him frustrated and angry, feeling that you have been unjust.

○ Give him the benefit of the doubt. Once you have told him something, let him get on with things and assume he is being responsible, without hovering obtrusively to see that he obeys you.

○ Be positive, telling him what he can do, rather than telling him "No!" all the time.

○ Be sure that you are setting him a good example. Why shouldn't he do what he sees you doing?

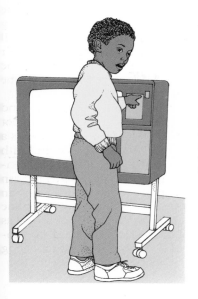

Most children go through a stage of testing their parents' authority, for example turning the television on when they have been told not to and looking to see what the reaction is.

'Crime and Punishment'

There are very few parents who have not lost their temper and smacked a child at some time, and when this happens occasionally it probably does no real and lasting harm. But smacking is never the solution to bad behaviour or disobedience. A smacked child often becomes so enraged and indignant that he can't remember what he had done wrong in the first place. And if you smack a child regularly for minor infringements, what will you do when he is really naughty? Getting into the habit of smacking can escalate into giving a real spanking later on.

Similarly, you must never punish spiteful behaviour with a smack. If your child has hurt another child, and you punish him by hurting him in turn, how can he possibly believe that hurting people is wrong? You would merely be reinforcing his spiteful or aggressive behaviour.

Humiliating a badly behaved child as a form of punishment can also have the wrong effect. If you put him in baby clothes or sneer at him because he is behaving 'childishly', you are simply exerting your power in a crude and aggressive manner, without any attempt to see why he has behaved in this way. His behaviour will probably have been caused by feeling upset, and treatment of this sort will only distress him all the more.

The traditional punishment of sending a child to his room, or putting him to bed early, can also rebound on his parents. It will make him hate going to bed, because every time he goes to his room it reminds him of his punishment, so his behaviour is likely to become even more disruptive.

So how can you exert and maintain discipline, when faced with a 'naughty' child? Firstly, you must establish whether or not the child is being deliberately naughty. He may simply have misinterpreted you, or have had a genuine accident. If this is the case, and he has been scolded, you must explain your mistake and reassure him, so he understands that you are not being unjust. If, on the other hand, he is deliberately being naughty to test out your discipline, you can't afford to let him win. You can tell him that he is just being silly, and that you are not impressed at all, but you should not physically punish him. Remember, try to reward good behaviour, and don't reinforce his bad behaviour by reacting to it as he wishes.

If he has been seriously naughty, such as stealing or being destructive, you must try and talk things out with him, to discover what is causing this behaviour. He may be upset, and making a cry for more attention, or he may be picking up habits from his friends. Until you know the underlying problem, you cannot decide how best to cope.

Don't feel guilty if you can't cope with his bad behaviour in a cool and rational way; it's only human to lose your temper occasionally. But try to see your child's point of view as well, before you scold, lecture or punish him. You want him to think that you were right all along.

○ By the time she starts school, a child should understand the concepts of right and wrong.

Behavioural Problems

How you define a 'naughty' child or a child with behavioural problems depends to a large extent on your own attitude to life, and your expectations from your children. If you are placid and happy-go-lucky, you may permit your children to run riot and not bother too much about it. On the other hand, if you value a quiet life, and like to preserve your home and its fittings, you may be perturbed by boisterous children whose behaviour seems to be getting out of hand.

Very often, the difficulties are not a behavioural problem at all, but are simply part of the child's development, exploring his environment, and learning how to fit into the social structure of our lives by trial and error. Because he doesn't yet understand the 'rules', he naturally breaks them, and so appears unruly.

When he plays with friends, you will have to remember constantly that what you find to be acceptable behaviour may not be so acceptable to another family, who will have established their own and slightly different set of 'rules'. It is not really fair to blame your child's friends for some minor infringement that would not worry their own parents. If there are major differences in the sort of behaviour that is tolerated, your child may find it more difficult to understand why he is disciplined differently than his friends.

Specialist help

Some children do have genuine problems, and these are often caused by emotional pressures. Such factors as broken homes, lack of parental love and affection, too-rigid discipline and fears and anxiety can all have a profound effect on a child's behaviour. Very often, the child cannot explain the problem properly, and the parents are too close to the problem to recognize it. Because they are often involved directly in the emotional upset which caused the behavioural problem, they may not be the best people to deal with it. In such cases, a child psychologist or social worker can often help, and the doctor may refer a disturbed child and his parents to them for counselling.

Lying and stealing

'Truth' and 'property' are two concepts that a child finds difficult to grasp, in the adult sense, because they are abstract ideas which are quite difficult to define.

Lying We all tell small lies routinely, such as denying that a small cut or bruise hurts, or may jokingly lie in such a way that our partner knows it is all in fun. But children don't think like this, and they have less of a direct grasp of reality. After all, a fairy story is a form of lie. It is presented to the child in a matter of fact manner, but is presenting a completely fabricated story as though it were fact.

Therefore, a small child cannot necessarily see anything wrong with telling a lie, and will often be bewildered at his parents' reaction. Most parents are more annoyed that he has told a lie than they were at the misdeed with which they challenged him. Faced with probable parental anger, most small children will lie without hesitation, because they think it may get them out of trouble. Although it may be hard to be reasonable when faced with a small defiant child swearing black is white, when you have caught him red-handed doing something wrong, it is only fear of your anger which is forcing him to lie. Try to be reasonable and avoid direct criticism of his behaviour, and he will see no need to avoid the truth; he may even confess to things you didn't know he had done!

Another form of lying is elaboration of the truth. This problem (which also affects many adults), is a form of fantasy, designed to make him seem more important than he really is. It is usually completely harmless and instances can be ignored or indulged, as you see fit.

Stealing A child's attitude to property is decidedly one sided, "What's mine is mine, what's yours is mine, too". As a baby he snatched toys from other children with impunity, and displayed little idea of personal property. As he gets older, he comes to understand the concept of sharing, but the idea of purely personal possessions is still difficult. Why is it, for example, that he can pick a flower growing beside the road, but must not pick the same sort of flower growing just the other side of the fence? Why can he bring home his drawing from playschool but must not take the pencil?

We all know the unspoken rules which define personal property, but they are difficult for a child to understand, especially within the home. He is surrounded by interesting objects, some of which he can handle without comment, while touching others cause his parents to become very cross.

However, there are times when you can be sure that he does understand the rules, and his acquisitive nature then leads to stealing. How should you react? Not by flying into a rage, because for any child under six years of age, you cannot expect to judge his actions by adult standards. It may be just a one-off experiment, in which case you must let him know that you don't like this sort of behaviour. But if stealing becomes a habit, especially when it involves people outside the immediate family, you have a problem which needs to be carefully examined.

There is sometimes an emotional cause to this behaviour. The child feels he is being deprived in some way, and is seeking to compensate. It may be that he is simply feeling deprived because you won't let him have something, so he steals it. Or he may be feeling emotionally deprived, because he is not getting enough attention, so he steals to provide himself with a comfort object.

It is important to control this sort of behaviour before it becomes established, and if you can't sort out the problem yourself, you should seek professional advice from a child psychologist, who you can contact through your family doctor.

Spiteful behaviour

It's very upsetting when another parent complains that your child has bitten or pinched their son or daughter, and its equally worrying when it happens to your own child. Your protective parental instincts immediately come into play, denying that your child would ever do such a thing, or being wildly indignant that any other child could assault your child in this way.

Most children go through a phase of spiteful behaviour, and most of them sort it out for themselves after a few tears and tantrums. When they realize that when they smack another child, he is likely to slap them straight back, they usually lose interest in that method of gaining their own way. You must be careful, however, if spiteful behaviour is directed at younger children, as bullying is an unpleasant habit which needs to be discouraged.

Often the spiteful behaviour will be directed at you. Kicking, spitting and screaming at a parent are all common aspects of frustration when a child cannot get his own way. When a child is behaving like this it can be difficult to love them, but this is what is needed, rather than physical punishment. If you smack them back, you merely let them know that this is the right way to behave, because even grown-ups do it. What you have to do is to let him know that his behaviour is offensive, but despite this you still love him.

Often the easiest way to get over an aggressive spell like this is to let him get his aggression out by running about and screaming or punching the furniture until he quietens down, then talking to him quietly and calmly to try to find out what was the root cause of his behaviour.

The boisterous child

'Hyperactive' is a term commonly used by parents to describe their boisterous child, and it is usually used by parents who have given up trying to exert any form of discipline. Used in this way, this is simply an excuse for having lost control of a child's behaviour and is an admission of defeat. In fact, true hyper-activity is quite unusual, and is a special behavioural problem (see pp.95–6).

The personalities of children vary widely, and some children are undeniably overactive. They are restless, fidgety, and are constantly off on new and interesting forms of distraction. Such children are usually very reluctant to go to bed, waking early and being generally difficult to manage. These are the children who go through the house like a small whirlwind, opening cupboards and strewing the contents on the floor while you are still

○ Outdoor activity is a good way for boisterous children to expend their excess energy.

attempting to clear up the mess from their previous raids. They are also the children who are most likely to be smacked by an exasperated parent whose tolerance has finally snapped.

An overactive child is constantly testing and pushing his parents to see how far he can go before he is checked. This behaviour is, in a way, a challenge to parental authority, and whatever he is allowed to do, he will always try to wheedle a bit more, just to try and get his own way. He will ask for "Just one more sweet", or "Can I just see to the end of this TV programme?", and when this always seems to work, he will progress to more demands until he finds he can do exactly what he pleases, because his parents are tired of checking him.

If you live in a small flat or room, having an overactive child can be a real problem, because one way to quieten down his behaviour is to encourage him to tear about and let off steam, and he won't be able to do this indoors. Take him to a local park or playground, and let him be as noisy and active as he wants. Let him play until you can see him slowing down, before you take him home and try to resume a more normal routine.

Stick to your routine as much as possible, and try to make your restless child keep to it too. It is important that he sees that there are rules in the home which cannot be broken, and that the household is not there solely for his benefit. You may get tantrums when he cannot get his own way, and these must be dealt with as they occur (see pp.96–7).

Give your unruly child a lot of attention, and build this time into your daily routine. If you involve him in some of your own activities you will be able to supervise his behaviour without having to say "No!" all the time. Don't give him time to go off and get into mischief, but keep him busy and occupied.

Don't expect too much of him. You *know* he's not going to sit still at the table, so there is no point in making an issue of it. Give him his meal separately, if you want to preserve the tranquillity of the family mealtimes. And never let him wander off in the supermarket or store, unless you want some embarrassing scenes with broken goods having to be paid for. You have to recognize the limitations on your activities that his behaviour causes, and make allowance for the extra supervision he will need.

Learning to fit into the family without causing disruption can take a child a long time, and you may need infinite patience before your boisterous child behaves in a way which you find acceptable. It is important that you sort out his behaviour while he is young and relatively compliant, because things would be much more difficult later on, when he is even more independent and defiant.

The hyperactive child

True hyperactivity is a behavioural disorder which resembles an extreme form of overactivity. Among the characteristics of a hyperactive child are restlessness and an inability to concentrate on anything for more than a brief period. He will also be irritable and prone to frequent tantrums.

Hyperactivity is a behavioural disorder which is so disruptive that it must usually be treated by a child psychiatrist and psychologist. Some people think that substances in the food may be at least partly responsible, and there is some evidence that a yellow artificial colouring called tartrazine or E102, which is widely used in drinks and foods, may influence the behaviour of children who are prone to hyperactivity. If your child seems to be overactive or even hyperactive, it is worth cutting out foods containing tartrazine, which is totally unnecessary to our diet, and added purely to make convenience foods look better.

It has also been suggested that some form of food allergy may be involved in hyperactivity, and elimination diets have been proposed, in which a series of foods are cut from the child's diet, while a check is made on the effects on his behaviour. A growing child does need a proper balance of nutrients so *on no account should you try an elimination diet without proper supervision from a doctor and dietician.*

If your child has a severe behavioural problem which might be hyperactivity, you must consult your doctor about it, because several effective forms of treatment are available.

Coping with tantrums

Tantrums are explosions of rage and frustration, which most commonly affect children between ages two and four. They are primarily done for effect, and a child will scarcely ever start a tantrum if he is on his own. They usually happen when the child is prevented from doing something he wants, and having tried wheedling and demanding, he then throws a tantrum as his ultimate weapon.

A tantrum only works because the parent is intimidated or embarrassed into giving way. A smack or other direct punishment only confirms to the child that he has succeeded in seriously upsetting his parent and provoking a response, so he knows that the technique is worth trying again.

During a tantrum, a child may seem to be completely out of control, and this can be very frightening for a parent. He may scream, kick, throw himself on the ground, and hold his breath until he turns bright red, and this can continue for half an hour or more, until he is totally exhausted. But despite its frightening appearance, he will never hurt himself – the tantrum is carried out for its effect on you, not to damage himself.

Some people cope with a child's tantrum by physically holding him until the tears and rage have died down. This can work, but is a harrowing experience for both parents and child.

As the tantrum is a demand for attention, it makes much more sense to keep away from him for as long as the tantrum proceeds. This does *not* mean shutting him in his room, which is a form of direct punishment. But if you walk out of the room, and noisily get on with the housework, the tantrum will usually subside

◌ Outbursts of tears and tantrums are an inevitable part of the growing up process.

often after a few pauses to check if you are really taking notice of him). Most children throw a few tantrums as part of their attempts to establish their independence within the family. If they discover it never succeeds, they soon abandon this as an unsuccessful technique.

Public tantrums

Handling public tantrums is a bit more tricky. We have all seen 'supermarket tantrums' and the effect these can have on a harassed and embarrassed parent. It's all too easy to give in and give the child a sweet or whatever else he is demanding rather than face the embarrassment of a howling child in a crowded shop. You can't very well walk away from him in a supermarket, as you would at home. The only solution is to abandon your shopping and leave the shop immediately, taking him straight outside and then home, and making it very clear to him that his behaviour has caused him to miss out on the treat you were planning *after* shopping. This is highly inconvenient in the short term, but giving in now would only store up problems for later.

PLAY

Learning and Playing

In very young children, emotional development proceeds at roughly the same rate, and through the same stages, so it is possible to predict what to expect from your child. In the preschool group, however, the child's growing independence and development of her own personality will affect the way she behaves and plays.

You can see this very clearly by watching how a child plays. All children learn by example, and play at being adults. They make up or re-invent universal games like 'Doctors and Nurses', or 'Mummies and Daddies', and will be totally absorbed in their complex play for many hours, even though they may seem to have very little power of concentration when you want them to do something else. But at the same time as re-living the reality they see around them, many children will make a deliberate effort to avoid doing what you expect of them, as a gesture of independence which demonstrates to them that they are not totally dependent on adults. This starts at the toddler age when most children demonstrate their independence by going through a phase of saying "no" to any question, but if you tell your older child that she is *not* to play in the garden, she will make a point of going there, to show you that she has a mind of her own. This is a normal stage.

Play is an absolutely essential part of growing up, and there is nothing sadder than seeing a child whose sparkle and fun has been crushed by being forced to concentrate on boring educational pursuits by well-meaning but misguided parents. Playing *is* learning, especially in an environment which encourages your child to exercise her imagination.

The stimulating environment

The child's environment consists of wherever she happens to be at any moment. If you sit her on a chair in an empty room, with nothing to look at, she will naturally become bored and irritable. In the same way, if her play environment is not stimulating, she will not be able to become involved in the complicated games which would help her to develop her social skills to the full. A 'stimulating environment' doesn't imply a 'Victorian nursery' with expensive toys and games, it is often the atmosphere created by you and your partner in the house. Allow your child to help with her ideas on how to decorate and create the place she wants to play in if possible.

This means that she must have both the place (such as her room or the garden) where her games can develop, and the props she needs for her play. These could consist of toys, furniture, trees, bits and pieces of apparently worthless rubbish which she has collected and treasured, and even yourself, if you are called on to take part in her game. If she needs you, remember that for the purposes of her game, you will no longer be Mummy or Daddy, but may be required to act out your play role with just as much enthusiasm as a child.

○ Many children enjoy playing in sandpits, but always ensure that they have not been fouled by cats or dogs.

Messy play

Children have little regard for cleanliness while they are playing, and you should be resigned to your child getting very dirty or wet, and dress her accordingly. You will also need to take some prudent precautions if she is playing indoors, putting vulnerable objects well out of reach. It is, however, useful to have one area where you don't mind what she does.

You will also have to remind her that this is your home too, and it therefore needs to be treated with a bit of consideration, even though this may mean making a little less mess, or transferring certain types of play out of doors.

Continuous play

Some games played by young children can go on for a very long time – even for several days – and they may bitterly resent being interrupted for meals or bedtime. If you see that play is developing in this way, it may be worth suggesting that all the props are transferred to her room or to some other part of the home or garden, so that they can be left undisturbed until after the meal, or ready for the next day. Play can sometimes continue through mealtimes, as you will see if your child has friends round for tea, or if they want to eat while they are 'camping' in the garden or in a corner of your living room.

Her play may seem pointless to you, but it is absolutely real to her. She will be completely absorbed in the characters she and her friends assume, and will resent your interruption in your parental role, which breaks this spell, and brings her back to mundane reality. The chair you move while you are tidying up may have been her car, and an old cardboard box a house. You won't know what is going on inside her head, and if asked, she probably won't tell you. So don't be in too much of a hurry to break things up to suit your own routine, but try instead to find a way for her play to continue without too much disruption.

Television and video

Television has a way of polarizing parents' opinions. On one hand are parents who look upon television as a convenient way to shut their children up, leaving them goggling at it for hours on end without consideration of the quality or content of their viewing. On the other are parents who regard television as a threat to family activities, to be viewed only occasionally and selectively, if at all.

The same arguments can apply to videos. For a tired parent, hire of a video for the evening guarantees an hour and a half of independence from children, who will be totally absorbed in their viewing. Or on the other hand, videos can be seen as 'moving wallpaper' which the children will watch without taxing their brains.

But are these relevant attitudes? Certainly television can be over-used, and if viewed in an undiscriminating way, can remove the incentive for a child to look and learn for herself. Similarly, it is foolish to assume that everything on the television is rubbish which should not be viewed unless it has a demonstrable educational content.

As with all such differences of opinion, the most satisfactory situation lies between the two extremes. Television is now an inescapable part of our society so, if you have one, it is unfair to deny your child some of the pure entertainment she can derive from viewing it. If she is not allowed to watch, you can expect problems when she finds out that her friends are free to view whatever they wish.

○ Free access to TV and video may make viewing hard to supervise.

Choosing suitable programmes

It is not difficult to judge those programmes which are suitable viewing for a child of any particular age, though you may have to be careful about those with a frightening or violent content which can disturb sensitive children. Programme schedules have carefully worked out the appropriate times in the evening when programmes suitable for a particular age group can be screened without serious clashes with bedtime. There is always a tendency for children to want to watch programmes intended for an older and more sophisticated audience, even though they may not understand them. This is part of their wish to be seen as more grown up than they really are.

You can usually avoid too many arguments by laying down a timetable of programmes which you think are suitable viewing and keeping to these as closely as possible. Above all, you must avoid unrestricted and uncritical viewing, which could be harmful to your child's emotional development.

Programmes on television or video which appear to be simply entertainment still have a valuable function for a growing child. They provide a broad picture of a world which is outside her normal experience, showing her other countries and societies, and giving her insights into situations which she has not yet encountered. Don't forget that a child still does not really grasp the difference between fantasy and reality, and don't hesitate to put her right if you see that she is taking some of the more imaginative material too literally, or becoming confused.

Handled in this way, television and videos become an important and controllable part of your child's growing up.

Creative play

By definition, play is a creative process. It involves imagination and the creation of an alternative reality, which for the child, is just as real as the world about her. Creative play takes many forms. It can be a complex game involving a number of children, all of whom cooperate to act out their roles according to a 'script' whose rules they understand without any prior discussion. Dressing up is an important part of such games, and you can encourage this by providing a bag of cast-off clothes which can be adapted for any need.

Other forms of creative play can be carried out by a single child, pushing toy cars around or dressing dolls. Some children do not interact well with others, and prefer to play alone in this way. This is fine, up to a point, but such children need to be encouraged to mix socially with other children, because this is an important part of their social development.

Imaginary friends

Many children have an imaginary friend during their early childhood, with whom they share their play and have long discussions. Some parents are extremely worried by this, fearing that their child has a mental problem. But this is a stage which most children go through, probably finding an imaginary friend to be much less demanding and critical than a real child. Often the child will act out problems which have bothered her during the day, telling the invisible friend the story of a minor incident from her own point of view, and often making her parents the villains of the tale. In this way, such imaginative play has a valuable function. It is certainly nothing for her parents to worry about; after all, you would not worry if your child had equally imaginary conversations with a doll or a stuffed toy. In time the child will grow out of this stage.

Creative toys

It is a good thing to encourage creative play, but difficult to do this without being intrusive. Children adapt what they find about them to make props for their games, and left to their own devices, need little adult assistance (unless they ask for it directly). The same applies to their toys. Most toys are bought because they appeal to parents, and in many cases these are over-elaborate for the child. Many toys which are very attractive for an adult are of limited interest for a child, because they can only fulfill the one function for which they were designed. They do not give the child any choice about the sort of game she can play. A toy vacuum cleaner can only be used for playing at cleaning the carpet, and a trumpet can only be blown. But dolls and Action Man toys are 'tools' which the child can use to take part in all sorts of other games, so they thereby stimulate many forms of creative play.

○ Construction toys bring out a child's creativity as well as improving his manual dexterity.

Toys and Games

When you buy toys (or improvise them) you should take several important points into account:

○ Cost

○ Durability

○ Safety

○ 'Fun value'.

Something that appeals to you because it is in good taste and looks well designed may be completely pointless for a child. She will be much more interested in how noisy it is, or how long it will continue to work before it breaks or the batteries wear out. Given a free range in a toy shop she will probably choose the pink plastic dog or the orange furry bear rather than the beautiful wooden puzzle you would have chosen.

If you buy toys from a reputable shop, safety should not be a problem, because there are strict rules about the materials and standards of construction used in toys. Beware cheap 'bargain' toys bought from street markets and stalls, if you don't recognize them as a well-known make. These could contain substandard and possibly dangerous materials.

Tips for choosing toys

○ Is it interactive; in other words, does it *do* anything in response to the child's actions? If not, she will soon become bored with it, and relegate it to a shelf or the back of the cupboard.

○ Is it safe to use, carrying a relevant safety marking? If not, check carefully to see if it seems well-made and finished. In particular check if there are any sharp edges.

○ If it is battery powered, are you really prepared to keep buying fresh batteries? Many battery toys run out after an hour's use, and it may be worth looking into the possibility of buying rechargeable batteries and a charger.

○ Will it encourage her to think, or be creative? This doesn't mean that the toy should be 'educational'; it must still be fun to play with, but it can stretch her a bit.

○ How robust is it? Never underestimate the power of a child to destroy toys in ways you could never dream of – even though you would not class her as a 'destructive' child.

Toys for a three to six-year-old come in all shapes and sizes.

Doll

Construction bricks and models

Tea set

Play mat

Toy telephone Cars Xylophone

Toys to consider buying

Soft toys Soft toys are a delight to most children, and will continue to be taken to bed long after they are no longer needed as a comforter. Don't ever try to 'break' your child of the habit of cuddling a much-loved soft toy, even if it is threadbare and disintegrating. It may provide her with comfort and security for many years, and will be a companion that she talks to and plays with. It's sensible to check occasionally that the eyes are still safely secured, and to wash it now and again.

Musical toys All children love noisy toys. Drums, xylophones, trumpets and harmonicas will all give her a great deal of pleasure. You might find the pleasure wearing a bit thin after a while though, as she will not get bored with the sound as quickly as you will. Try to encourage her to develop a sense of rhythm so she can learn from her play and noise-making (see p.116).

'Wet toys' Water fascinates children, and you can encourage their play by providing a small paddling pool. Don't put too much water in it, and supervise play at all times. Many sorts of other games can be played in the paddling pool or in the bath, or standing on a chair at the kitchen sink. An assortment of plastic jugs and bottles will provide hours of fun, pouring water from one side to the other.

Tea set The tea set is a great stimulus for realistic play, and is especially useful in getting a group of children used to playing well together. Use safe plastic tea pots and cups, together with spoons and plastic cutlery. There is no need to produce real tea, milk or sugar, and it will be less messy if you let your child use her imagination!

Modelling clay Encourage games which allow her to express herself. Modelling clay such as Plasticine is an excellent plaything. It encourages creative playing, squeezing the clay into shapes, cutting it, and mixing different colours. Making recognizable shapes from modelling clay is just as creative as painting or drawing. Unfortunately clay quickly gets very dirty, because it picks up fluff and dust, so you will have to replace it occasionally.

Fitting stabilizers onto a bicycle will make it safer while a child makes the transition from a tricycle.

Bikes and trikes Depending on the physical size of your child, she can safely play on a tricycle or a bicycle with stabilizers to prevent it from tipping over. If it has a chain drive, you must make sure that she appreciates the danger of getting fingers pinched if she meddles with it. At about age five some children are ready to start learning to ride a bicycle without stabilizers. If she doesn't seen to have enough balance and coordination yet, leave it until later on, and leave the stabilizers on for a while. Be very careful once she is riding her bicycle properly, because as well as the risk of falling off, bikes of this type travel quite fast, and a child can shoot out into the road very quickly. Remember that her enthusiasm for speed will outstrip her common sense, and don't let her ride anywhere dangerous. Don't buy bicycles which are too large and could be uncontrollable.

Dolls and figures All children love to play with dolls, or with miniature figures, which they use in many creative games. Dolls and figures can be companions, and they also encourage speech development, giving a child someone to talk to. Children tend to be fascinated by small dolls, so don't assume that the biggest and most expensive doll you can find will always be appreciated. They can use tiny figures in other games, fitting them into dolls' houses, garages and toy cars. If your child does have the traditional larger dolls, try to provide plenty of clothes for dressing-up games.

Puppets Like dolls and small figures, puppets encourage creative word play. A child can quickly learn to use a glove puppet, but string puppets quickly become tangled up and cause frustration.

Writing and drawing Writing and drawing is a valuable part of learning. Try water-based felt-tipped pens, crayons and also wax pencils. Be very careful that any pens you give her are washable, and check to see that they are marked 'Non-toxic', in case they are chewed. Lining paper bought as a roll from a decorating shop is the cheapest paper, and one roll will last for a long time. See also pages 112–115.

Puzzles These can help a child to think logically, and identify shapes accurately. Don't buy puzzles that are intended for older age groups, or you may make her frustrated and cause her to lose interest. Jigsaws are usually favourites as are old-fashioned metal puzzles, consisting of small pieces of twisted and entangled wire. Don't buy puzzles which have many small pieces which will inevitably get lost. Keep all the parts together in a plastic box.

As a child gets older, she can manage to manipulate smaller and more intricate jigsaw pieces.

○ Children emulate adult roles when they play with dolls.

Games Simple card games like 'snap', 'happy families' and picture lotto and, once she can count, board games like snakes and ladders, are good because they encourage play with others.

Construction sets These are now made in a variety of different shapes, from the familiar building bricks like Lego to more unusual interlocking shapes. All will help coordination and manual dexterity. Many also feature small figures, animals or vehicles so that a whole scene can be created.

Telephones A toy telephone is a wonderful toy, stimulating speech practice, and forming part of many other games. Just make sure that your child knows not to use your real telephone though, or you will have some very expensive bills.

Tents and camps Building houses, tents and camps seems to be a universal game among all children. All they need is a stack of cardboard boxes and old curtains or sheets, and they will devise games which go on for hours or even for several days. They can draw windows and doors on a box, and it becomes a house or a shop. Sheets and curtains can be draped over a clothes line or across furniture, to become a tent in which a child can hide for hours. Alternatively, you may wish to buy a commercial wendy house, or build one.

Clothes Rather than throwing out old clothes, necklaces, hats or shoes, put them in a box as dressing-up clothes. They will provide stimulation for hours of pretend play. Face paints and masks are equally fun.

Books for Fun, Books for Reading

Books *are* fun, and it is impossible to have too many of them. Some parents worry about their children becoming 'bookworms', preferring them to take part in physical play, sport or outdoor pursuits. For a few introverted and shy children, this can be the case, and they use books as a substitute for learning to cope with the complexities of real life.

For most children, books, like television, provide a window to the world about them, although unlike television, three- to six-year-olds are not able to understand more than a few words of the printed text. But almost all children are fascinated by pictures, and love being read to. They do not tire of having their favourite story read and re-read to them, time and again.

At first, you provide her only real access to what is in a book. She cannot understand anything about what is in it, until you help her, but once she gets the idea, she may make up her own stories to suit the pictures. If you ask her what the pictures mean, she will be challenged to put her imagination to work and will derive as much fun from making up her own story as she does from the story you read to her (although this is a developmental process and you shouldn't expect it much before $4\frac{1}{2}$ years).

A child who is used to having plenty of books about her at an early age will continue to read well at school. She will already be familiar with letters and words, and will have memorized many even if you have not deliberately attempted to teach her to read.

Even before he can read, a child will be able to make sense of picture books, and understand a story read to him.

What type of book should you buy?

Don't worry about buying books with an educational content, because there is plenty of time for this when she starts school. At this age, *all* books are educational, whether for reading from, or just looking at them.

By age three or four, your child should have developed some understanding that books are fragile, and you may need to teach her not to tear pages, or to scribble on them. Books can be expensive and easily damaged, but a child does not seem to notice if her favourite book is disintegrating and will still cling to it for many years.

Comics can also be fun for children and teach them to follow a story through a sequence of pictures. She will find this useful when she actually starts reading.

○ Children never seem to tire of hearing their favourite stories.

Painting and Drawing

Painting, drawing or just plain scribbling are ways in which a child can express herself, as well as being fun. At first, a child is simply fascinated by the marks she can make on the paper, and by colours. The ability to draw a recognizable face or a whole man develops quite quickly, and by age five she will be including quite a lot of detail in her drawings of the human form (see pp.16–20). It is not long before a picture has to be made in such a way that it tells a story. If you ask a child about a picture she has drawn, she will be able to tell you a complicated story about the picture, just as she can invent long and complicated games when she is playing with her friends.

Block painting

Painting need not be confined to the brush technique. Your child will be able to produce more interesting results if you give her a variety of objects for block painting. Cut a sponge in half and let her experiment with dipping it into the paint, then onto the paper. All kinds of familiar household objects are good for this, such as an old cotton reel, a toothbrush or a cork. When you go for a walk, get your child to look for other objects that she might use, such as a fir cone or acorn.

Spray painting

A further variation your child may enjoy is to put a blob of paint on the paper, then blow through a straw so that the paint 'sprays' out into a pattern. Provided you are using non-lead-based paints, she won't come to any harm if she accidentally forgets to blow and sucks instead.

Hand and foot prints

For finger or foot painting you will need to make the paint thicker than usual. Adding a little flour to powder paint will achieve this.

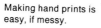

Making hand prints is easy, if messy.

○ Paint brushes are quite difficult to manage, so early pictures are often abstract splashes of colour.

○ Modelling clays can be moulded into all kinds of shapes and reused again and again.

Experimenting with different textures, such as a sponge, makes block printing more interesting.

Equipment

It just isn't possible for a young child to be creative with paint without making a mess so the most important pieces of equipment are plenty of newspapers or dustsheets to cover the painting surface and surrounding area, and a plastic apron for your child.

If you want (and can afford) an easel, it will make an ideal prop for painting. Many have a tray at the bottom to hold the paint pots. You will still need to supply newspapers to cover your flooring in case of accidents. However, if the weather is fine, why not pin the paper to a fence or the side of a shed outdoors?

When you are buying paints, the best type is the powdered variety. You can then mix up exactly the amount your child needs for each painting session. You don't have to buy a whole rainbow of colours – with blue, red and yellow you (or your child) can mix any colour she wants. Young children tend to paint monochrome pictures to begin with so there is no need to supply more than one or two at a time.

Other craft activities

Once she has mastered the art of producing a drawing that is recognizable (to her), she will take great pride in drawing objects you suggest to her. Encourage her to extend her play to other forms of communication. She can cut out pieces of paper (under careful supervision) and paste them onto her picture. She can also make shapes and figures out of modelling clay or plasticine. The latter is harder for a child to use because it is stiffer, especially when it is new.

Get into the habit of saving kitchen roll tubes, egg boxes, shoe boxes and other items that can be glued together to make models. (Always provide non-toxic glue only.) If your child doesn't use them at home, her play group or nursery school will probably be glad of them.

Music

Everyone seems to have a built-in sense of rhythm, and you will notice this when you see a toddler jumping about or skipping approximately in time to a piece of music with a powerful beat. Obviously a young child cannot appreciate the sophisticated complexities of Bach or Mozart, but she will listen and derive pleasure from music that she hears on the radio or from your stereo. She will also pick up the idea of dancing spontaneously.

Making music and singing follow naturally from listening to music. A small child cannot sing on key or follow a tune for more than a few bars, apart from a very few prodigies. This is a learned ability, which takes a long time to develop. She will enjoy making sounds with simple musical instruments. Singing, however, is much easier, because the voice can be more readily controlled than a musical instrument. Almost all children can sing along with simple nursery rhymes, and many can play back simple jingles from television commercials, which are often equally simple. Action rhymes and songs are also popular with young children.

You can encourage your child's interest in music by giving her a simple (cheap!) battery radio or tape to play with. She may listen to it incessantly, but unlike single-mindedly watching television, she will be able to spare part of her attention for other things. Cassette recorders are relatively child-proof too, and give her the choice of music to listen to. Even small children quickly learn to use the controls of a cassette player or radio in order to listen to programmes or music that they enjoy.

Few children can resist the temptation of banging on a drum.

Blowing across a partially filled bottle will produce musical notes.

Hobbies and Pastimes

The three to six age group may seem a bit young for hobbies, but even at this age many children have developed particular interests. Collecting is a universal interest for small children. They will collect small and apparently worthless items, such as pebbles, conkers, and dead (or sometimes living) bugs in matchboxes, and will make a tremendous fuss if you attempt to clear these away.

Other children develop an obsession for watching cars or trains, or for cooking. These are all aspects of a developing personality, and they often provide an indication of the sort of approach to life which will follow. A toddler fascinated by cars will often develop an interest in mechanical things as she grows older, while the child who enjoys skipping to music at age three or four may well develop more formal musical interests later.

○ A first catch is a big moment for a novice angler.

Enjoying Pets

Caring for a pet can help a child develop a sense of responsibility. Small pets such as hamsters, gerbils and goldfish are suitable for young children, but they will need supervision to make sure that the pet is not accidentally mistreated. This type of pet is completely vulnerable to the person caring for it, and even a responsible child will need to be watched to make sure that no harm comes to the pet.

Rabbits, guinea pigs and cats are more suitable pets, because if they are mauled about too much, they will bite or scratch and run off. At the same time, they are large enough for a child to handle without accidentally squeezing them. If you have a pet cat, don't forget to get it wormed regularly.

○ A young kitten is irresistible for a child.

Feeding and caring for a pet will foster a sense of responsibility in a child.

Just as with very small children, dogs should not be trusted unsupervised with the preschool age group. Dogs have a strong sense of their own importance within the family group, and regard a boisterous toddler or older child as a threat to their status. Even the most placid dog can turn on a child, especially when rough play gets just a bit *too* rough. Children love dogs, and will play happily with them for hours, and there is no reason to deny them this pleasure. Just make sure, especially with large dogs, that there is no possibility of playful nips getting out of control, and that the child realizes that most dogs could bite if provoked too much or accidentally hurt. Like cats, dogs need regular worming so they do not spread disease.

If you have a cat or a dog you should be especially careful about cleaning up after it. Cats in particular will sometimes use a child's sandpit as a litter tray. This exposes the child to the risk of toxocara, which in extreme cases can lead to blindness.

Birds are less satisfactory pets because they are not usually handleable, being too small and easily hurt. A child will take little interest in a pet she cannot handle or play with.

You may feel that bringing up a small child causes you enough work without having to clear up after a pet. But this could rob your child of the possibility of learning to be responsible for another individual, and of having a playmate for some games.

Even if it is not practicable for your child to have a pet, you can still encourage her to take an interest in animal life. She may enjoy feeding the birds in your garden, or you could take her on regular trips to the local lake or river to see the ducks. Point out when the birds are nesting, then return to see the newly hatched ducklings, then again to observe how they have grown.

Most children will enjoy a visit to a farm. Even inner-city areas often have small farms that welcome visitors. Such a visit may be the first time your child has seen sheep, horses, chickens and other farmyard animals, apart from in books.

The Benefits of Healthy Exercise

Exercise is just as valuable for a child as it is for an adult, but for slightly different reasons. For the child, exercise has several valuable functions:

○ Exercise lets off steam, and uses up some of his surplus energy.

○ It improves his coordination and strength. A child used to plenty of exercise learns to use his body properly, and is less liable to trip over and be generally clumsy than an inactive child of the same age.

○ Exercise improves his health, because it builds his muscles, gives him a good appetite, generally tones up his system, and gets him outside.

From his parents' point of view, his exercise is good for them too, because they can relax while he is tearing about. But probably the best form of exercise is one that can involve the whole family. Swimming and walking are family pursuits suitable for individuals of almost any age, and both are excellent exercise. Remember that your child's strength and stamina are not that of an adult, so he could get overtired. A young child on a long walk

○ Learning to swim with the help of inflatables is good exercise and equips children with a potentially life-saving skill.

will often not admit that he is getting tired until he has reached the point of exhaustion and becomes grizzly and bad-tempered, so you must match your family exercise to his physical abilities.

You can also start him off on ball games and sports which will improve his coordination. Catching a ball is difficult for a three-year-old, but this is a skill which rapidly improves with practice. At first, ball games are taught by parents or older children, but once he is able to interrelate and cooperate with children of his own age, he will be able to play with them. You or another adult will probably have to referee their ball games to head off the worst of their disputes.

Catching a ball is a difficult feat for a three-year-old because it requires good coordination and timing.

At five years of age a child can throw a large ball with reasonable accuracy.

Throwing is probably easier for boys than girls, perhaps because their forearms are slightly longer.

Play Groups and Toddler Nurseries

Play groups and nurseries can help your child to develop her play skills in a way which can be difficult at home. However much you encourage your child to play with others, she is still aware that she is in her own home, and her play will therefore be influenced by this knowledge.

In the playgroup or nursery, she is away from your supervision, and can play freely with other children, under the watchful eye of another adult. It is not fair to expect a young child to fit into a group of children without some prior experience of mixing with others, so you will still have to encourage her to play with friends at home. She may object to being left, too, and you will probably need to stay with her at the first few sessions until she is confident enough to take part in all the activities.

Children as young as 18 months to two years derive pleasure from play groups, although at this age they play alongside one another rather than together. Nevertheless, they are important in the development of social interaction. For older children, they provide valuable opportunities for 'letting off steam' and being as noisy as they like, while giving their parents a welcome break and opportunity to meet other parents and make new friendships.

Most play groups only take children for short periods each visit, and a couple of hours is usually sufficient for younger children. It is also long enough for you to catch up on chores or pursue your own activities, once you are satisfied that your child is happy and will not fret.

○ One benefit of play groups is that children join in group games.

○ In a play group children learn early social skills through interaction with playmates of a similar age.

Finding a play group

These groups are usually privately run, often by groups of parents, and you can get in touch with one by asking your health visitor, or by checking the notice board in your corner shop or library. They are usually heavily oversubscribed, and you will have to put your child's name down for a place very early on.

When you are thinking about taking your child to a play group or nursery, it is wise to check it out thoroughly and ask yourself some key questions.

Points to consider when choosing a play group

○ Has the nursery or play group been recommended to you by someone whose child already attends?

○ When you visit, do all the children seem happy?

○ Are there adequate play facilities, with plenty of toys available?

○ Do you feel you can trust the people in charge to look after your child?

○ Thinking back to your own childhood, would *you* have enjoyed this nursery or play group?

EDUCATION

Nursery School

By law, a child must begin school no later than the start of the first school term following their fifth birthday. (In Australia the age varies according to the state or territory, but the latest age is six years.) This is the latest possible date, but it makes a lot of sense to start your child's education earlier, if at all possible. He will find his first sessions of full-time education quite tiring, and very strange, and attendance at play groups, nurseries or nursery school can help him to adjust to the new situation.

A nursery school is operated by the local authority, unlike play groups and nurseries, for which a fee is usually charged. There is a distinct difference between the two types of schooling. The play groups and toddler nurseries exist primarily to care for children and to encourage them to socialize and play together (see pp.122–3), while nursery schools and classes run by the local authority are usually slightly more structured, with the objective of preparing children for full-time education.

You will have to make enquiries locally about what facilities are available. Nursery education is available in most towns, but in some rural areas or in deprived areas, you may find difficulty in locating a suitable school.

Just as with play groups, you will need to check out any nursery class or school very thoroughly, and prepare your child for it before sending him off to full-time education. Many preschool children seem very self-confident and cocky, able to tackle anything – so long as Mummy or Daddy are there to back them up if things go wrong. A confident child can be very distressed and deflated if things don't go all his own way at school, and you need to prepare him as much as possible.

Check it out

Visit the school yourself and look around, talking to the teachers, and especially to the person who will be in charge of your own child. You must be happy and confident in their ability to care for your child as you would yourself. Ask to watch the children at work and at play, and look to see how problems, such as tears or 'loners', are handled. You will need to be sure that there is adequate supervision during outdoor play, good play equipment, outdoor trips and visits. You should also find out if parents are encouraged to participate in school activities.

Face the problems

It is unlikely that you will find a school that seems perfect in every respect. Indeed, many parents do not succeed in getting their child a place in nursery school, due to a chronic shortage of places. You may have to accept a compromise, placing your child in a school where you foresee some potential problems. You will have to balance these against the benefit to your child of socializing and playing with a large group of other children. For example, class sizes may be larger than you would like – but see if this seems to be having a bad effect on the children already in the class. Your child might be one of only a few of his ethnic group in the school. This does not necessarily cause problems, but you should discuss with the teachers or organizers how they cope with any problems which could arise from this. Religion and special dietary requirements may also be a consideration here.

Get him prepared

Teachers and staff at the nursery school will often suggest ways of preparing your child, so he does not have too many shocks when he starts school. Let him know, for example, if you will be staying with him for a while, or if he will simply be left at the school. Once he knows what will happen, he is less likely to be distressed at finding himself 'abandoned' at the school door.

Try not to send him off to nursery school near to the birth of another baby, or he will feel that he is being pushed out of the way, and you can expect jealousy later on.

Make sure he has a 'conducted tour', so he knows where the toilet is, and what the lunch arrangements will be. He will probably be much too shy to ask, and needs to be told that it is alright to go to the toilet when he needs to. Of course, you will need to make sure that he is capable of going to the toilet unattended by the time he starts nursery school, and you must tell the staff if you think he may need help, or if they can expect some accidents.

Another thing which worries a child left at nursery school for the first time is that his parent may not collect him. Make sure that he knows how and when he will be collected or met, and make arrangements with another parent to take care of him if ever you are delayed – and tell him who that parent is. He should understand that he must *not* go off with a stranger, and that if anyone bothers him he must tell his teacher or another adult.

First days

In many nursery schools, you will be able to stay with your child, at least for a while. Do not prolong this period of protective care, because you are preventing him from integrating into the group, and acting for him so that he will not gain his independence. Once you are able to leave him, he will soon be able to adjust and make friends.

Expect him to be tired and irritable when he gets home, because he will be both physically and mentally exhausted until he adjusts. Don't worry if he seems uncommunicative about what has been happening – he probably needs some time to sort out his own attitude to school and won't want to talk about it yet.

At the end of his first day at school a child will probably be pleased to see a familiar face.

Even if he is enjoying himself, your questioning may seem as though you are still trying to keep an eye on him, and robbing him of his independence. When he does start to tell what's been going on, show your interest, and especially give him encouragement for his first painting and models.

It is wise to arrive to collect him quite early, and to let him know that you will be there before he comes out of school. Arriving late just once can cause him to panic and feel abandoned.

Early problems
If he tells you that he hates school, don't take his tears too seriously. He could simply be checking to see if you still love him, making sure that you are not just getting rid of him by sending him off to school. You can encourage him to enjoy school by telling him about boring things at home – but *don't* tell him about interesting activities you may have been doing, because that would make him feel that he is missing out. Your objective must be to make him feel sure that school is the best possible place for him to be.

He will soon start to tell you about some of his new friends, and you should encourage his new social contacts by telling him to ask them round to play. Check with their parents first because a child of this age will have no idea of the worry that can be caused if they wander off without telling someone.

Helping with Education – or Interfering?

The reason for the five-year deadline for formal schooling is that educationalists have found, from experience, that this is the optimum age to start teaching in groups. Before this age, children are unlikely to have the self-discipline and concentration to work together for any length of time.

Teaching methods and attitudes towards learning vary widely, and some teachers like to think that when a child first begins school, he has no preconceived ideas about basic skills, such as reading or addition and subtraction, so the teaching can proceed from fundamental principles.

If your child is interested you can help him recognize words by using flash cards, but do not push him.

Word skills

Any parent who reads regularly to his child knows that although not yet ready for formal education, he takes an interest in the written word. Once the child realizes that a particular shape on the printed page means a particular word, he will search out that word and repeat it back – he has understood reading, and begun to learn it for himself.

When you read to him from children's books with large, clear print, he will have little difficulty in identifying words, and will quite soon be able to 'read' alone, repeating back familiar words to himself. If you want to encourage his interest in words and reading, you can help him along by buying or making flash cards; pieces of card on which common words are printed in large, clear text. You can ask him to sort through these and select a particular word you have asked for. Do not confuse the apparent ease with which he recognizes and repeats words with proper reading. He is merely recognizing shapes, not the letters and sounds making up the word. He may actually correctly identify the word 'Grandma' because it has a smear of jam on it, rather than because it begins with the letter 'G'. Despite this, many children can read simple words well before they go to infant school.

Even an ordinary outing, such as a visit to a local pond, can be a novel and educational experience for children.

Learning through play

Even though you may not be aware of it, you are preparing your child for school by introducing different concepts into his everyday play activities. Playing with water, for example, as well as being great fun, can teach a child that some objects float and some sink, and that different-shaped containers may be filled with the same amount of water.

In the same way, conversation is a key factor in the development of a child's learning, so involving your child in discussions is vital. Not only will it help his own speech, and later his reading and writing, but it will also teach him about ideas. For example, a simple question like "Where are your blue shoes?" will help him learn about colours, while "Please pass me the smallest book" will encourage him to make comparisons.

Sorting objects such as buttons by colour, size or shape will help a child learn about counting, weight and texture. A young child will have to be supervised to make sure he doesn't swallow any.

Formal teaching at school is usually quite different, an teaching your child letter sounds yourself may conflict with th of the school and cause confusion. Your child may be surprise that there are other ways of looking at words which he alread knows quite well, but if he has a basic understanding of wh reading is for, and how it works, he will have an in-built readin advantage when he starts school, which will undoubtedly hel him for many years.

Writing and arithmetic are other areas where schools may hav particular methods, and your attempts at teaching could caus confusion later. There is no harm in teaching a child to count o his fingers, or to add up by counting piles of building bricks, bu it is unwise to go much beyond this preliminary stage.

Telling the time is one simple way for a child to get t understand numbers, and you may be able to teach your five year-old how to read the time to the nearest hour or half hour. H will not understand the intricacies of 60 minutes to the hour unt much later, and has little real sense of the passage of tim However, there will be clocks in his school, and it will be helpf to him if he has some idea of when to expect lunchtime an finishing time.

A child will learn to tell the time more easily if can associate his everyday activities with particular times.

At school pupils begin to learn about subjects, such as arithmetic, in a more formal way.

Getting Ready for School

By age five, your child is feeling pretty self-confident. He is physically agile, usually aggressive and cocky, and is able to express quite complicated ideas. If he has been attending nursery school he will be one of the older children, able to take charge in games and to get his own way with younger children. All this is about to change.

The day he starts his infant school, he will find that he is now one of the youngest and least significant children there, and that almost every other older child in the school knows more and can do things better than he can. It's not surprising that many children get anxious in their first few days at infant school, and some are fearful at the prospect of starting. It's up to you to make the transition into this school as painless as possible, so he can get on with the business of getting down to some serious learning.

Peer group pressures

It will be important for him to fit in well with other children, so you should help him to conform as much as possible. Children of this age are not able to cope with feeling different from their fellows. For example, you can rethink some of the family slang. Most families have a number of 'private' expressions used as euphemisms for going to the toilet, or for other routine activities. Many of these are continuations of childish mispronunciations.

○ A child will listen more attentively and respond to storytime in class if he is used to hearing stories at home.

which are still used because they are amusing. But a child may not realize that these are part of a private 'family language' and will be humiliated when their new friends mock them for asking to "Go wee-wee" or "Do a poo". Make sure that he knows and can use the appropriate words or expressions for every situation he is likely to encounter.

A child's wish to conform also extends to his clothing. Watch the other children and see what sort of clothes they are wearing. Your child will feel very self-conscious and out of place if his clothes are drastically different from those worn by the other children. If the school has a uniform this problem will be solved for you.

If your child is to slip comfortably into the school routine, there are a number of basic skills and abilities he will need to be competent at. He should be able to cope confidently with the following everyday activities.

Skills to be mastered before starting school

○ Being able to say both his names and address clearly.

○ Dressing and undressing himself.

○ Tying his own shoelaces (don't worry if he can't).

○ Putting on his own gloves, and being responsible enough to put them in his coat pocket so they don't get lost. (If this is a problem, attach them to elastic and thread this through the sleeves of his coat or jacket.)

○ Washing his face and hands thoroughly, especially before meals, and drying them properly afterwards.

○ Using the toilet without supervision, flushing it properly, and washing his hands afterwards.

○ Blowing his nose properly and hygienically.

○ Using a knife and fork, and eating reasonably tidily.

○ Being adventurous enough to try meals which are different from those he normally gets at home. (Prepare him anyway.)

○ Sharing his toys and games with other children, and clearing up afterwards.

○ Being trusted enough to be responsible when you are not there to keep an eye on him.

At school your child will have to change for sport and other activities so he should be able to dress and undress himself unaided.

If your five-year-old can cope with all of these things, both you and he are to be congratulated. In practice, very few five-year olds will be ready for school without any preparation, and you may have to concentrate on some of these points so as to make life as straightforward as possible for him when he goes to school.

Choosing a suitable school

Selection of the new school should follow much the same procedure as that outlined on page 123 for the choice of play groups and nursery schools. However, in some areas your choice may be limited by the local authority, and your child may be obliged to go to a particular school. In addition to the general points to be looked at, there are a number of specific questions relating to the way the school is run which you may like to ask the staff when you look round (see opposite).

Don't be afraid to ask questions like this, and make sure you get satisfactory answers. Probably your most reliable guide to the general quality of a school can be obtained by talking to other parents. All schools have a local reputation, which is the consensus of opinions from many people.

Supplying information for the school

Once you have made the decision and are ready to register your child with the school, you should be prepared to be asked many questions, some of which may seem rather personal and over-detailed. But it is important for the school to know about your family's religion, whether or not you work (so you can be reached if there is any emergency), if there are other children, or if you or your partner are unemployed. The school needs to build up a complete picture of your child's family background, because it can affect his behaviour and his educational needs.

If there are special domestic situations which could affect your child, you should tell the school about them. Such things as separation or divorce, or the death of a member of the family can

Assessing a school for your child

○ Are the children grouped by age, or streamed by some other means? If so, what does this mean in practical terms for the children?

○ How many children are there in each class?

○ Do the children stay with the same teacher throughout the school, or does the teacher change every year?

○ How is a child's progress assessed? Will you have access to the assessment?

○ Would the teachers class the school as 'progressive' or 'traditional' in terms of teaching methods and discipline?

○ Is there a parents' association or its equivalent?

○ What is the school policy towards lunches? Are they prepared on the premises, or can packed lunches be brought in? Are mealtimes properly supervised?

○ How much access do you have to teachers if and when problems arise?

○ How well equipped is the school?

○ A tour of potential schools is useful in assessing the classroom activities and facilities of each school.

cause upsets which are carried over to affect the child at school and the teachers need to be alerted to any possible problem, or the need to be specially sensitive.

The last night before starting his new school will probably be a time of great excitement for your child. He will have packed and repacked his bag several times, and will probably be both apprehensive and over-excited. A hot bath and a warm milky drink may help him relax, but don't make too much of a drama about his new school, or he will never settle down.

○ Starting school may be a bewildering experience, but a child should soon settle into the school routine.

Problems at School

Despite your careful preparations, it is quite likely that your child will encounter some problems at school, especially during the settling-in period.

Anxiety

Do not despair if your confident and cocky five-year-old emerges from school in floods of tears at the end of his first day, and possibly for several days after that. This is not necessarily because he does not like what is going on in the school, but more because he was unprepared for it. However much you describe to him what the school routine will be, his imagination will be limited by his lack of experience, so he will find it all a shock, particularly if he did not attend a play group or nursery school. He will never before have been faced with several hundred children, most of whom are bigger and pushier than himself, and he won't be prepared for the sheer noise and bustle of a large school. Faced with this situation, a quiet word with the teacher can help. Teachers are used to dealing with all sorts of emotional upsets, and can give your child some special attention if he really requires it.

He may express his anxiety in less obvious ways, such as reverting to sucking his thumb, bed-wetting or even throwing one of the tantrums that you thought, and hoped, he had abandoned years ago.

If your child takes a particular fancy to another child's property she may need persuading to return it.

Stealing

Don't be surprised if your child comes home from school with some small item that doesn't belong to him, and expect a few of his own belongings to go missing as well. Children of this age do not have an adult sense of property, and certainly do not understand the concept of stealing. All you need to do is to explain to him, calmly but firmly, that this is not the way to do things, and insist that *he* gives it back to the other child or to the teacher. Don't make a big drama of it, because this is probably a one-off incident, which he won't want to repeat. Habitual stealing is more of a problem, which you will need to discuss with the teacher, so it can be stopped before it develops into too much of a habit.

Bullying
Serious bullying does not usually affect the youngest children, who are generally well supervised at school. However, some older children make a point of pushing the new children about, just to establish their authority (most of us did this ourselves), and if this happens, your child will become understandably upset. If your child doesn't want to tell you, you may hear about it from a friend. Try to find out exactly what has happened, and if you think it is more than an isolated incident, have a discreet word with the teacher. Try not to discuss the incident too much in front of your child, as this could blow it up out of proportion to its actual seriousness.

Perhaps even more of a worry is if it is your child doing the bullying. Always be aware of this possibility, and if you see or hear it happening explain in a loving way that he has to stop. If it goes on a tougher approach will be needed.

Teasing
Children will often make remarks about the personal appearance of others, sometimes just as frank statements and at other times to be intentionally cruel. If your child has a physical defect, such as protruding ears, a disfiguring birthmark or a stammer, he may be subject to this sort of teasing when he starts school. Although you can't protect him from unkind remarks, you can talk to him about it so that he realizes that everyone is different and that he has no need to worry about his appearance. Assure him that the teasing will stop in time if he fails to react to it. This is an important part of preparation for school so don't forget it as all our children have some special weaknesses or problems.

Truancy
True truancy is a deliberate and prolonged absence from school, and this is a problem usually restricted to older children. If a five-year-old disappears from school, it is usually only because he is frightened and wants to come home, rather than going off to play with other truants. In a well-supervised school, it should not be possible for a young child to leave the premises unexpectedly, so if this happens, see the teacher and try to sort out the problem.

Right-handed or Left-handed?

Writing with the left hand is not a problem so long as the child holds the pen comfortably in such a way that he does not smudge the words with his hand as it travels across the page.

About one in ten children are naturally left-handed, and although this concerns some parents, in practice it does not cause any serious or lasting problems. The most significant result of being left-handed is that his writing will be extremely awkward and untidy. Many left-handed children turn the page sideways so they can see what they have written without it having been obscured by their hand, or hook their hand over so the pen points down towards the bottom of the page for the same reason.

Outdated prejudices

Older people in particular sometimes insist that a child should be persuaded to write with their right hands, because this used to be the practice (it still is in many Mediterranean countries). However, left-handedness is cause by a difference in brain development between the two sides, so changing sides can be very difficult. There is some evidence that forcing a child to become right-handed may be associated with the development of speech problems such as stuttering, or of behavioural disorders.

Reassuring your child

Don't let a left-handed child think that there is anything wrong with him, because there isn't. Remember that in any large school about a hundred children are left-handed, and they all cope perfectly well. He may have a few minor difficulties like learning to tie a knot in his shoelaces, and he may use his knife and fork in the 'wrong' hands – so what!

The Clumsy Child

Some children seem just 'born clumsy'. However much they are nagged and scolded, they are always the ones who knock over their drinks, accidentally pull the table cloth off when they leave the table, and fall off their bikes at least once a week.

There may be a reason for this, and rather than laughing it off, it is worth discussing the situation with your doctor, clinic or health visitor. If, as is usually the case, there seems to be no real reason for your child's clumsiness other than his physical enthusiasm outstripping his coordination, there is nothing to worry about, because he will eventually grow out of it as he learns to control his body.

Being left out

Clumsiness can sometimes cause problems at school if it persists. A child who is not well coordinated will not do well at ball games and other pursuits involving physical skill, and will soon feel out of things when he is not invited to join in with other children or is the last one to be picked for a team. If he is conscious of his clumsiness, because of teasing by other children, as well as nagging by his teacher and parents, he will naturally become anxious and withdrawn. Discuss the problem with his teacher, because there will be some activities where he can shine, without his clumsiness interfering. Explain this carefully to him and just encourage him with what he can do.

Playground games are an enjoyable part of school life for most children. However, a clumsy child may feel inhibited from joining in physical games.

Gifted or Precocious?

We all like to think that our children are extra bright, and take pride in their achievements, especially when they manage these at an earlier age than other children. Parents brag about the achievements of their babies and young children just as much as an angler will boast of the size of the 'one that got away'. Usually the child is totally normal, and the parent has just seized on some small aspect of his behaviour which differs from other children of the same age.

Some children are actually much more intelligent than their fellows, but this is not always realized by their parents, or later, by their teachers. A young child who keeps asking "Why?" can be very irritating, and may be simply demanding your attention by his questions, with no real interest in the answers. But for a very intelligent child, these questions are meaningful and he really wants an answer.

Precociousness

Do not confuse precocious behaviour with gifted behaviour. Many children mimic adult behaviour very skillfully, but this is usually done without any real understanding, and is not a measure of their intelligence.

Once at school, a high level of intelligence can sometimes cause problems, unless it is recognized and the child's teaching is adapted accordingly. The gifted child may differ from other school children in a number of ways.

Signs of a gifted child

○ He may be isolated from other children, because he is not thinking at the same level, and cannot therefore take part in their play.

○ He may become frustrated and suffer from behavioural disorders, because he realizes that he is different and cannot relate properly to other children.

○ Other children may shun or tease him, because they resent his over-achieving in class work.

○ He may deliberately *under-achieve*, so he is not embarrassed by standing out from his classmates.

○ He may be disruptive and badly behaved in class, because he is bored with lessons which are not demanding enough.

○ At home, he may be aggressive and over-active. Gifted children sometimes seem to need little sleep, compared to others.

○ A genuinely gifted child may find lessons too easy and consequently become bored.

Some teachers and educationalists believe that all children should be taught together at the same level, while there are other arguments in favour of giving special teaching to gifted children. There is no easy answer to this problem. Special treatment can certainly provide the level of mental stimulation needed by these children, and reduce the level of frustration they experience in 'ordinary' schooling. But often the minds of gifted children seem to be directed too much into one or two narrow areas. They become obsessively interested in a few subjects, and are seldom 'good all-rounders'; this is one of the arguments for continuing their education in a normal school, where they are encouraged to interact with other children in all the school activities.

If you believe that your child may be gifted, and that this gift could be affecting his schooling, you should first discuss the situation with his teacher, and possibly also with an educational psychologist. Not all areas make special educational facilities available for gifted children, and if you are committed to this, you may be forced to seek private schooling, but get good advice.

Children with Special Needs

Many children have special needs at school. Sometimes these are based upon emotional factors. A family divorce, unemployed parents, or a bereavement in the family are all problems that can affect a child badly, so they need some special care from teachers or those looking after a play group.

Other children may have some physical problem which demands some special care and attention if they are to progress to the best of their ability, and to take a full part in all the school's activities.

The child with learning problems

Inability to learn Probably about three per thousand children are profoundly retarded and need special care and treatment for their entire lives. It is usually obvious and there are many different causes, both genetic and environmental, for severe learning difficulties. Many other children are, however, only affected in a minor way, and are able to attend ordinary schools, although they may need special attention or remedial teaching in certain areas.

'Normal' intelligence spans a very wide range, and people who are at the bottom end of this range will experience some difficulties in learning.

An inability to learn effectively is not necessarily anything to do with intelligence. A physical defect such as poor sight or hearing affects the ability of the child to learn, as does an inability to recognize words properly, as in dyslexia. It is important that parents and school identify the underlying reasons for a child's learning difficulties, in order that the correct remedial measures can be taken. This usually means a preschool assessment with an educational psychologist who will attempt to determine your child's capabilities, and help with his particular requirements.

Once a delayed child is ready to attend school, it is very important that teachers are advised of the situation, in order that they can deal properly with difficulties which could arise. In particular, they will need to make sure that the child does not suffer in his interactions with other children, who can be unthinkingly cruel to a child who is 'different'.

Education has to be matched to the needs of the child, and children who are only slightly slow are usually able to cope with normal school life, even though they may need some special teaching. In some cases, there may be special units within the school, or they may need to attend some special classes in different schools. Generally speaking, if the doctor, the educational psychologist and the school feel that a delayed child will be able to cope with school life, then he will be better off there than in a special school where he will not be able to mix with children who are not affected. He will also be assessed at regular intervals to see if his placement is continuing satisfactorily.

Children with visual defects A child with a serious visual handicap will already be receiving special care (hopefully), but there are many children whose sight is only slightly impaired. The problem should be picked up during routine health checks. For a few children, the problem may only become apparent once they start school, and begin to experience some learning difficulties. They may not be able to see words chalked up on a blackboard which is some distance away because they are short-sighted; or they do not learn to write properly because they are long-sighted and cannot focus properly on the page in front of them. The problem with most children is that they will not tell you. If you are concerned about vision, or if there is a strong history in your family of visual problems go and discuss it with your doctor or health visitor. Vision is so vital for a child to learn.

Once minor visual defects are identified, they can usually be rectified with spectacles or some other form of treatment, and then they no longer act as an impediment to the child's progress at school. Wearing glasses does introduce a few problems in play and sport, but most children quickly adapt to wearing them without any difficulties.

If a child cannot see his teacher or the blackboard he will find learning difficult, so it is important that any visual defects are picked up early and rectified with glasses or other treatment.

Squint Another reason to contact your doctor straight away is if you think your child has a squint. Have it checked immediately. It can be remedied and is important as an uncorrected squint can lead to one eye taking over from the other eye and can cause the loss of three-dimensional vision. Squints tend to run in families so look particularly if you or your partner had one as a child. It can affect a child if other children tease him about his condition so discuss this problem with him if he appears to be anxious (see p.138).

◊ Hearing aids allow many children with impaired hearing to enjoy a normal life at school and at home.

Impaired hearing Inability to hear properly can make it difficult to learn. Impaired hearing or total deafness can be caused by damage due to infection (for example German measles) while still in the womb, to a genetic defect, or to some other form of damage to the brain or nervous system. The most common cause is, however, fluid in the middle ear – a condition known as Glue ear. It is caused by a long-standing infection. This particularly affects a child's ability to hear low sounds like 'ball' or 'bath'. Again if you suspect a problem or if there is a strong family history get your child checked early.

Children with impaired hearing are often very noisy themselves, and they develop speech later and less fluently than children with perfect hearing. At school they can suffer by not hearing what the teacher is saying, or by confusing instructions they have been given. They are often disruptive and badly behaved, purely because they cannot participate fully in class.

Special facilities are provided for profoundly deaf children, but those whose hearing is only partially affected can often use hearing aids which allow them to take part in normal school activities and learn normally.

Children with Minor Handicaps

There are a number of handicaps which may need to be taken into account when a child is starting school. Some of these are very minor but can still be disturbing to a child. You may find it helpful to join a parent support group who will be able to give reassurance and advice about the condition. Your doctor should be able to give you the names of relevant organizations.

Speech impediments Stuttering, stammering, or lisps, do not affect education directly, but they can cause a child to become embarrassed and withdrawn. Children with speech impediments are often teased by their classmates, and they may be reluctant to respond to their teachers or to other children for fear of being mocked. Most speech impediments respond well to therapy, so affected children should not find their impediment causes lasting difficulties, but in general the earlier treatment is begun the better. It will usually mean referral to a speech therapist by your doctor. Stammering is more common if other members of the family stammer.

Any physical handicap is distressing for a child, who will always wish to conform to what he sees as the 'norm' for other children. There are also some forms of handicap which are less apparent, but which can be very disruptive to a child's school life.

Autism This is a mental condition which causes a child to become withdrawn and unresponsive to other people. Autistic children become completely involved in the world within their

○ Schools should have facilities, such as ramps for wheelchairs, to cater for disabled children.

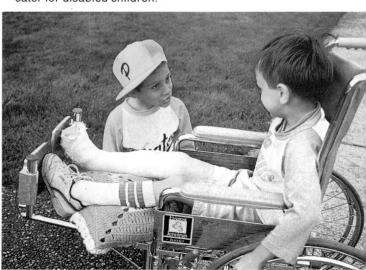

own brain, shutting out their parents, teachers and other children, and playing apparently meaningless games with themselves for hours on end. Sometimes they carry out ritualized behaviour, such as hand clapping or rocking to and fro, or they may wander off and stare into space for long periods.

There is a lot of confusion about this condition. Lots of children are withdrawn at certain times of their life but this isn't autism. Many retarded children have some 'autistic' features, but again this isn't true autism, which is a serious condition needing proper psychiatric evaluation and treatment. An autistic child will probably always need special care, because he will find great difficulty in participating fully with his schoolmates.

Epilepsy Children with epilepsy also experience difficulties, but these are mostly to do with the way in which other people react to them. Epilepsy is a condition in which the brain sometimes sends bursts of incorrect signals to the muscles, causing a fit or convulsion. This is very frightening to an onlooker, but the affected child recovers afterwards with no recollection of what has happened.

If a child has frequent fits, he may need to attend a special school. However, most children with epilepsy have their condition well controlled with drugs, and are able to go to school like any other pupil. There are certain types of activity, such as swimming or climbing, which have to be restricted, as they could be risky if a fit occurred.

Teachers must always be warned about the condition, and know what to do if the child has a fit. Dealing with the attitude of the other children is not so easy. They will be alarmed if they see a fit taking place, and unless the situation is properly explained to them, the affected child may find that he is treated differently from his fellows, and made to feel an outcast.

Epilepsy is quite common, and simply means a tendency to recurrent fits. A child is not classed as epileptic after one fit. In fact any of us can have a fit; it just depends on what sort of stimulus is required to trigger one. There are probably one or two affected children in any large school, with their condition properly controlled and not apparent to others. Not all affected children have major fits with muscle twitching; there is a minor type of epilepsy in which a child appears to have been 'switched off' for a few seconds, being completely unresponsive or sometimes moving a limb uncontrollably. This is known as Petit Mal. It is important for the child's teacher to be aware of it as it can interfere with learning if it happens frequently. This type of epilepsy often improves as the child gets older.

BACK TO WORK

The Parents' Roles

For every family one of the most important questions to consider is who should have primary responsibility for the child during the day.

The working mother

Deciding on when (or if) to go back to work can be difficult for a mother. Like many other decisions, it means balancing up the points for and against working. It is also a question that you may have to re-examine periodically as your circumstances change.

If you are on a tight budget, or if you are alone, you probably won't have any choice – you need the money, so you have to go back to work. You may be climbing the steps of a competitive career and just can't stop for five years (plus) if you hope to remain in the field. You may also enjoy work and value the stimulation, so are reluctant to stop for too long. There is no reason why you should not combine work and childcare but it isn't easy. Local authority childcare facilities are poor in most areas and finding suitable alternative provision can be expensive and time-consuming.

Deciding whether to return to work

○ If returning to work for financial reasons consider how much you will earn once your childcare has been paid for.

○ Can you organize adequate childcare for your child/children by the time you need it?

○ Will your child enjoy being away from you? How can you prepare her for it? For example, gradually build up the amount of time she is away from you.

○ Do you feel guilty?

○ Are you being pressured into work?

○ How does your partner feel about you going back to work?

○ Will your job allow you to take time off if your child is sick?

○ Do you have any back up if childcare breaks down, even for one day?

○ It is difficult to organize work and childcare – can you cope with the hassle? You may have to compromise on one or both.

Provided you can sort out in your own mind the answers to difficult questions like these, there is absolutely no reason why you shouldn't go back to work with a clear conscience. Most mothers do work now, and manage perfectly well. In fact, it has been shown that a child's development directly relates to her parental wellbeing. If a mother is depressed through isolation and frustration her child won't be getting optimum stimulation. Many child minders and day nurseries are excellent, and in many ways a child gets more opportunities by being looked after by more than one person, provided the childcare is well planned. But if you can't convince yourself that you have addressed all these points satisfactorily, you may find yourself worrying, guilt-ridden and not giving your paid job the attention it deserves.

You may be able to get part-time work which allows you to be there at the school gate when your child leaves in the afternoon, but if not, you may be able to make some arrangement with your partner or another parent to look after your child until you get home. You will need to leave a telephone number with the school where you can be reached if there are any problems, and you may be able to recruit grandparents, friends or relatives to help out in an emergency if you can't be there yourself.

Try not to work immediately your child has gone to nursery school or infant school. Give her a week or so to settle down, or she will assume that you have packed her off to school to get her out of the way, so you can go to work. Even if this *is* the case, you won't want to upset her by making it too obvious.

The working father

Bringing up a child is hard and if it can be a team approach you will both stay calmer. Many fathers find it difficult to spend enough time with their children. In order to give a child the parental love and attention she needs, the father has to plan his daily timetable just as carefully as the mother, and needs to allocate some specific time for playing with his child.

If you get home late from work, you probably arrive just as the evening wind-down is getting underway, with bathtime and evening stories. So when you get in, tired and hungry, you may have little time for anything other than a goodnight kiss. Are you sure this has to be the case every evening? Perhaps at least one night a week you can be sure you are home early and devote all your time to your child. There is no reason why your child shouldn't take up as much energy as your work. Obviously a balance is required but you can't escape the fact that children do change your life and demand attention.

Sometimes, especially if your job involves commuting, you will get in very late. But if this is the case, playtime can be made up at the weekends. You can make a special point of taking your child out for a special treat, leaving your partner to get on with some of her own leisure activities.

○ A minority of fathers are now taking primary day-time responsibility for their children by looking after them at home.

The important thing is that the child appreciates the role of her father in bringing her up, and does not think of him as a stranger who she only gets to talk to at weekends.

Father as childcarer
An increasing number of men are choosing to stay at home and take primary care of their child while their partner goes out to work, or are forced to do so due to redundancy or unemployment. Although this situation may be ideal from the point of view of both parents and the child, because it is still not the norm it can cause some minor problems. The feeling of isolation may be particularly acute when all the other childcarers seem to be mums and it may take longer to be accepted into 'mother and baby' social groups. However, the rewards more than compensate for this.

Who Looks After Your Child?

All-day nurseries

A few local authorities (and it really is a few) run day nurseries which give priority to parents who are in real need of someone to care for their child. There are very long waiting lists for these nurseries, and your desire to go back to work does not usually classify as a priority, unless you are a single parent (see also p.161) or have a handicapped child, or have some other pressing social problem.

To get a place at a council day nursery you usually need to apply to the social services department, and your needs will then be assessed by a social worker. (In Australia, you should apply to the local council.)

Getting your child a place at a private nursery is usually much easier, although you will normally have to pay some contribution towards the care given to your child. Some guidelines towards selection of a nursery are given on pages 123 and 134–5.

Creches

A few enlightened employers provide facilities for nurseries or creches at the place of work, either free of charge or at a competitive rate. This practice is very much more common in other European countries, but is slowly growing in popularity in the UK. If you know that several people at your place of work would welcome these facilities, it may be worth discussing the possibility with your employers.

Child minders

A child minder is a person who is (or should be) registered with the local authority as being suitable to care for a specified number of children in his or her own home. Registered child minders are supervised and their premises are inspected, so the facilities and care they provide are usually of a good standard. However, there are many unregistered child minders about, and if you use one of these, you will have to ask yourself whether he or she can supply the sort of care you want for your children.

You can contact registered child minders through your local social services department – they should have a complete list of all the child minders in your area, and you may be able to find someone to recommend one or more of them. Child minders also advertize, although the demand for childcare is so great that few of them have any difficulties in filling all their places.

The best possible child minder is the one who is recommended by several other parents, on the basis of their own experience. Bear in mind, however, that all children are different and respond in varying ways to particular personalities. It is therefore important to find a child minder who will relate well to your child. Here are a few pointers to look out for, when you are trying to find the right person to look after your child.

Child minders/nannies at home

Some childcarers will come and look after your child in your own home. This has many advantages but do work out in advance how much money you will allocate for food, and discuss the heating arrangements and the use of the telephone. Keep strictly to times of childcare and don't forget it can be difficult if you are at home for some reason.

Many families find it convenient and cheaper to share a child minder. In many ways it is a good compromise.

Au pairs

If your child is at school or nursery and you work full time you may find the arrangement of a live-in mother's help or au pair practical and worth considering. If you work a standard seven-hour day, you will need someone to pick your child up from school and entertain her for up to three hours a day. You can't rely on friends for this amount of time on a regular basis. Don't underestimate how difficult it can be to share your home with someone, but it can work out very well.

You should also bear in mind that many au-pairs are young and may have little knowledge of children. Don't give a teenager too much responsibility with your precious child.

Guidelines for choosing a child minder

○ Do the children seem happy? Make sure you visit the child minder when there are actually children there, not just in the evening. Does he/she really like children?

○ How many children will the child minder be supervising at any one time?

○ Are there adequate play facilities? Is there adequate room?

○ Have you made sure you know exactly what you are getting for your money? What about hours, illness and holidays?

○ Are there any special problems or requirements that the child minder should know about?

○ Do you feel that this is a person whom your child will get on with well?

○ Is the child minder registered? Has she been personally recommended to you?

○ Combining paid employment with bringing up children leaves many mothers little time for household chores.

Making it Work

Make no mistake about it; going back to work is not easy. You will be swopping a full-time job of caring for your child for another full-time paid job, while you still have the responsibility of caring for your child. At the same time, you will have to cope with possible problems from a child who may feel she is being pushed out of your life, after having been the centre of your attention for so long.

But it's not all bad. Most children cope very well when both their parents are at work. In fact, for many of them, it is great fun to be mixing with children all day, instead of being on the fringes of an adult world. It may make them value the time spent with you more. And however much you love your child, you will probably feel a great sense of freedom if you are able to think about other subjects for some of the time.

You can make the transition between being a full-time parent to being a full- or part-time employee much easier if you approach it in a methodical manner.

Organizing the home front

○ Plan your daily routine so you and your partner can allocate time for housework, shopping, *and* caring for your child.

○ Expect some tears and tantrums when your child realizes that you have some other interests in life, and don't let her panic you into thinking that going to work is not such a good idea. She will soon get used to the idea.

○ Give your child lots of love, affection and attention when you are with her.

○ Get plenty of rest (if you can!). You will find it a strain trying to cope with the extra work, but don't let household chores get on top of you.

○ Make a contingency plan. Make sure that the school, nursery or child minder knows how to get in touch with you if things go wrong, and tell them how to contact another responsible person if you are sick or cannot collect your child.

○ If you can afford it, use some of your new earnings to buy yourself some labour-saving items, such as a microwave cooker, washing machine or tumble dryer. These will all help you by saving time.

FAMILY LIFE

Establishing Your Own Life

However much you love your child, you owe it to yourself and your partner to make sure that you still have a life of your own. It is very easy to slip into the situation where your entire day is filled with caring for, and worrying about your child. This happens gradually. When you have a new baby, of course babycare is the biggest thing in your life. But you may find your routine begins to revolve around the baby, instead of the baby being fitted into a routine that you find convenient. Of course, setting up a routine does not work like this at all, and you will have to make many compromises in your personal life at first.

Because you love your child, you naturally want to spend as much time as possible with him. At first, you will need all of this time, because if it is your first child, you will be uncertain and lack confidence in what you are doing. But you must realize that children have to develop their independence, and need more and more time to themselves as they get older. Rather than hovering anxiously and fussing around at all times, encourage this growing independence and use it in a positive manner so you can begin to build up your own interests again. You do not own your child. He is an individual in his own right and so are you.

A preschool child can be very demanding of his parent's time and attention, and he may need encouraging to play with other children while you get on with domestic jobs or other pursuits.

Finding time for your partner

You will naturally value the time you can spend with your partner in the evenings, but there is no reason why you should not have a regular evening out on your own, leaving your partner to care for your child. Similarly, you must make a real effort to get out with your partner, leaving your child in safe hands with a baby-sitter or friends. It is easy to postpone social events because it is too much trouble to find a trustworthy baby-sitter, or because you fear your child may play up. Do this, and you will gradually lose your friends, and when your children eventually do lose their dependence on you, you may find that you don't have a social life any more.

Friends and a social life

You may find it convenient to cultivate friends who have children themselves, so your child can go along with you, and the children can play together. This is fine, and it is a relatively strain-free way to maintain your social contacts. But it doesn't get you away from your child or from childcare, and every couple needs some time together in privacy, where they can talk and enjoy each other's company.

○ Grandparents may be happy to look after your child for short periods, giving you some free time to spend with your partner.

Don't let your partner feel squeezed out of your life because you are continually concerned with your child. Many women lose interest in lovemaking after the birth of a child, not because they are frigid, but because their whole attention is devoted to their baby. Most men tolerate this situation for a while, then begin to feel left out and frustrated. If the mother is too tired to want to go out in the evening, or goes to bed early because she is tired, just after he gets back from work, tensions will be introduced into the partnership which can eventually lead to arguments and worse.

Parental privacy

The presence of a growing child in the house forces some changes in the way his parents behave towards each other. Almost all parents speak about private matters in 'code' which they imagine their child will not understand. In practice, most children know very well what their parents are talking about, because almost as much of the message is conveyed by tone of voice and body movements as is conveyed by the words themselves. So parents are always inhibited in their personal conversations, and this makes normal communications a little strained.

In almost all modern houses, poor sound insulation means that it is possible to hear noises from other rooms, and many parents are particularly conscious of this when lovemaking. It is difficult to give your full concentration to your partner when you are listening for small footsteps on the landing outside, or are hoping that any noises won't wake up your child. In fact, most children are not at all bothered by their parents' lovemaking, even if they happen to wander into the bedroom at the wrong moment.

It is wise to tell your child that your bedroom is your private place, and that he should, out of politeness, knock before coming in. The effects of such interruptions are much worse for the parents than for the child. Children do not feel embarrassment at other people's personal activities, although they may be curious about what is going on. The parents, on the other hand, are often consumed by guilt and feel (incorrectly) that they may have scarred their child for life.

If you think that as well as caring for a child, you are still leading a full and fulfilled life, ask yourself the following five questions.

Are you just a parent?

○ Are you still carrying out some of the hobbies, pastimes and social contacts you had before you started a family?

○ Do you ever give your partner your *full* attention?

○ Has your love life deteriorated since you had a child?

○ Do you feel guilty if you go out without your child?

○ How are you going to feel when your child doesn't want to go out with you and your partner any more?

If your answers to any of these questions suggest that you have been neglecting your own life, it's time to sit down with your partner and work out the best way of putting the situation right.

Getting your Rest

Most parents of young children complain that their children wear them out. An active and demanding child seems to need very little rest himself, and caring for him will be mentally very tiring; even more tiring if you have to play football or other strenuous games with him too.

Childcare is tiring and is often a bit tedious, and it's even more exhausting if you have to go out to work as well. You will need adequate rest if you are to cope. Rest is not necessarily the same thing as sleep. We all adjust to the amount of sleep needed by our bodies every day, although this varies between different individuals. We sleep soundly at night, and can make allowances for the occasional late night or interrupted sleep. But getting adequate rest is somewhat different.

Breaking up the day

We all need short breaks during the day, when we can 'switch off' mentally and relax. If you are at work, you value short coffee breaks and lunch time, because these are when you can relax and forget about work for a while. If you are caring for a child, you are working just as hard, if not harder! You certainly need these breaks in just the same way, and you should make allowance for these in your daily routine.

Set aside just a few minutes to relax with a cup of coffee and the paper during the morning, or sit down and watch the television for a while after lunch, just to let yourself unwind. If you are out at work, and you have to cram all your housework into the evening, make sure you stop for a short break instead of working yourself into exhaustion.

Even a five-minute break can make you feel better. Your child may not want to cooperate, and will probably try to interrupt your break. He will not understand your need for peace or privacy, so unless he is old enough to understand when you explain it to him, you could try starting him off on some activity which he can manage on his own, like painting or playing in his room with a friend while you take a short break.

It is a good idea to get into a practical routine, allowing yourself rest periods, then try to stick to it as much as possible. However, if you feel too tired, leave the housework or other non-essential chores for a day or so.

The Single-parent Family

More than one million children in the UK are now brought up in single-parent families. Usually this in not from choice, although more and more women are choosing to start a family without having a permanent partner. Some single parents are men who have lost a partner through divorce or bereavement, and are raising their child themselves.

Financial problems

Almost all single parents have one major problem, which is money, and most single-parent families have to manage on less than half the income of a two-parent family. This often means that the children of single parents are deprived in certain respects. They may be deprived of some material things, such as new clothes or toys, or may be brought up in substandard housing. They may also be deprived of parental attention, because the single parent is *forced* to go out to work, even when this is not desirable from the child's (and parent's) point of view.

If you are a single parent, you will need to investigate what benefits and assistance are available to you. In the UK, Child Benefit and often, Family Income Supplement is available, and your Social Services department will be able to advise you about how these should be claimed. In addition, in some areas, help with housing may be provided. In Australia, you may be eligible to receive Family Allowance or the Family Allowance Supplement. Contact the Department of Social Security to see how to claim assistance.

Finding childcare

The most difficult problem is getting someone to care for your child, if you are in an area where there are few day nurseries. Children from single-parent families are often given priority for places at nurseries, but if no publicly funded nurseries are available, the cost of private care can be prohibitive.

It is always worth seeking out local self-help groups, such as Gingerbread, (see pp.207–9). You can contact such groups through your doctor, welfare and social workers, community noticeboards, or through the local 'grapevine', by talking to other parents who are in a similar situation.

Time for yourself

It is easy to become isolated, so you need to make special efforts to find friends and develop other interests. It is often useful to arrange with another parent to 'swop' children on a regular basis, so you can have time off to get on with other things.

The situation is not all bad, however, because being a single parent can mean that you develop an even closer and more loving relationship with your child than in a two-parent family. You can make your own decisions, and you can be completely independent.

The Failed Partnership

A large number of marriages fail, and so do many partnership between unmarried couples. It is not the process of divorce which causes the worst upsets with children, so much as the unpleasantness which leads up to a final split. Children are very sensitive to atmosphere, and they will have seen arguments and tension building up towards the final break in a partnership.

Coping with divorce

The child's loyalties will be divided, because however fair you try to be, each parent will want to keep his love and affection, and will be competing to retain this. A young child is incapable of choosing between his parents, and will not understand the implications of all that is happening to him and his family. His world is literally being torn apart. Many children also feel responsible for the break up. They remember the times their parents argued about them. You should therefore be aware of this, reassure your child and keep doing so, accepting that even then he may not believe you.

Faced with the break-up of his family, most children react with behavioural problems. They may resume bed-wetting, spiteful behaviour, or become extra loving. Often their play with other children is affected, as they take out their frustrations on playmates, and if they are old enough to be going to school, their work will suffer.

The actual process of divorce introduces many other problems. During this time-consuming and difficult period, the child may feel that the parent who is caring for him is neglecting him, making him miss the other parent all the more. The courts primary concern is for the well-being of the child, and this does not always mean that the mother is automatically given custody, although this is generally the case.

The question of access to the child is difficult. In most cases the parent who is separated from his or her child will have a legal right to access, but too much right of access in the early days can make the process of settling down with the other parent more difficult. These problems need to be resolved by the court and by social workers, and the child's future must be carefully considered.

Creating a new life

After the disruption of a divorce, it is important to plan how your life and that of your child will continue. It will take some time before your own life can settle down to a routine, and it may also be a long while before your child can feel secure and loved again. Working out with your former partner such things as maintenance, access to the child, and division of belongings and possibly, a new home can reduce the worry and responsibility you feel as a new single parent.

If one of the parents walks out on his or her partner and child and severs all further contact with the child, he will inevitably feel betrayed and upset. He may find it more difficult to relate to any new adult, feeling that they may leave him as well. He may also feel that it is his fault that his parent left and blame himself if the remaining partner is upset.

A new family

About three-quarters of divorced people remarry or set up home with another partner, and when this happens, it means further upheaval for the child. He will have to adjust to a new family which will almost certainly have different 'rules' from the ones he was used to. If he has been living alone with one parent for some time, he may view the newcomer as a rival for his parent's affections and treat him or her with open hostility. You should discuss possible problems frankly with your partner before setting up house.

One of the first problems to be faced is whether or not he should call your new partner "Mummy" or "Daddy". He will probably be quite familiar with your new partner, and will have decided for himself what is the best thing to call them. Your former spouse will also probably have strong views about this, and if you are still on reasonable terms, it is worth discussing this to avoid difficulties during access visits. Try and put the welfare of your child above personal pride or your natural need to please your new partner. If your child is confused and anxious about points like this he is unlikely to accept your new partner readily.

A new partnership may mean moving to a different home. This is a difficult time for a child anyway, as it often means losing his friends, but when this coincides with the permanent installation of your new partner, you must take pains to make sure that the new partner is not blamed by your child for all the changes that are taking place in his life.

Step-brothers and step-sisters

Often your new partner comes complete with a new family. Step-brothers and sisters are often welcomed as new playmates, but you should expect there to be squabbles and jealousies especially in the first few months. It will also be a long time before your child ceases to take sides. He will almost certainly run to his natural parent for comfort rather than to a new parent. This can be hurtful for both parties, and it is important to realize the difficulties your child has in forming his new allegiances. If your partner has children from a former marriage, don't forget that they too have the same difficulties. You will have to try to make family life fun for all of you – it may help to start off with a holiday together.

Family Activities

It's very easy to let your whole world revolve around your child and his needs (real or imagined). It's also quite easy to find yourself feeling a bit resentful about the amount of time and attention your child takes up, especially as he gets older and ever more demanding. Some parents find that their children are the primary cause of their arguments.

In fact, it's best not to spend too much time thinking about yourself, or about your child, when you should be thinking about all of you together as *the family*, a unit which lives together, and enjoys life together. If you stop to consider, there are very many activities which you can all enjoy equally, instead of persuading yourself that you enjoy helping your child play a game which you actually hate.

For a child any time spent with her parents is potential playtime, even a shopping trip can be more fun if it involves a piggyback.

Outings

Try to be positive about family outings, some of which will cost you nothing. Walking is healthy, and it's fun, even though some children raised in a car-riding society may need a bit of persuasion to persevere with it. Take a ball along to kick about if they get bored. Similarly, swimming and bicycle riding are good family pursuits. You don't need to concentrate only on physical pastimes. There is nothing wrong with settling down together to watch television or a video, and it's far better to watch as a family than it is to switch on and leave a child watching alone, using it just as an electronic baby-sitter.

Visiting historic buildings and museums, or other 'educational' trips should not be neglected, provided you find them interesting yourself. A lot of what he sees there may go over a child's head, but he will still find enough to occupy him, though you will have to answer a lot of questions about what he sees.

○ Picnics can be a fun family activity.

Joining in with adults

Let your child participate as fully in your family life as he seems able. Though at first you may need to exclude him from the meal table when you have company, let him join in once you know he can fit in, and *if you think he will enjoy himself*. The key to keeping the whole family happy together is to do things that each member of the family will enjoy. If someone has to force themselves to look as though they are enjoying what you are doing, then you probably shouldn't have bothered. Next time, try and find something else to do. An adult may be prepared to suffer if he is not enjoying himself, but a child certainly won't, and he will grumble and groan and spoil things for the rest of the family.

For the child of keen gardeners, having a little plot to tend herself makes her feel part of the family and she will be delighted when any of her plants flower.

Holidays

By age three, children understand holidays and enjoy them enormously. Once a child is out of nappies it is very easy to take him almost anywhere, and you no longer need to feel many doubts about taking them abroad, if you can afford it. The need to be constantly entertained is less for a small child than it is for an adolescent, because the young child is constantly stimulated by exploring his new temporary environment and finding his own things to do.

Before you go on holiday ask your doctor whether your child will need any immunizations and, if so, arrange for them to be given in good time.

Easy travelling

Travel is the biggest problem when you take a small child on holiday. It is unreasonable to expect a child to sit still and quiet for long periods, whether in a car, train or aircraft. Similarly, children do not understand the need to prepare themselves for a long journey by going to bed early the night before, and taking pains to use the toilet before they set off. So long journeys can be a bit of a strain, with the need for frequent stops for using the toilet, eating snacks and having drinks, and letting off steam. This is all very well if you are travelling by car, but not so easy if you are in a train or travelling in an aircraft. You can play 'I spy' games and other simple pursuits to distract his attention during boring motorway driving, when there is not much to see, but it is better to plan your journey in such a way that he is less likely to become bored.

○ Booster seats enable young children to use seat belts in the back of a car.

To make the journey easier for the child, yourself, and other travellers, take plenty of things to keep him occupied. Books and games are useful, but make sure that games don't contain lots of loose pieces that are likely to get lost and that reading doesn't make him carsick. The best way to eliminate boredom is to make sure that your child actually wants the books or games you take along to entertain him. Take him out shopping with you to buy them, and let him choose something he wants for himself. You should explain to him that they will be saved for a day or so, and that he will have them as soon as the journey begins. This way, he anticipates and enjoys the journey.

It is a good idea for any child to realize that he must sometimes be patient if he wants something good. The journey on holiday is the 'patience' and he has to learn to cope with it. It is the same principle as encouraging a child to watch a seed grow. It may take months, but if he can learn to wait he will be proud of his flower when it appears.

At the resort

When you are at your holiday destination, be prepared to relax the rules a bit. You can indulge him in some of the treats that are rationed at home, and let him stay up later, if he's not too tired. This is one time when you don't need to battle over bedtime and food, and giving in over small things for a couple of weeks won't do any harm – provided you make it very clear that things go back to normal once you get home again!

Eating unfamiliar food can be a problem, especially with foreign holidays. Many children are extremely suspicious of anything they haven't tried before, but most hotels and guest houses have a children's menu, and children's favourites, such as chicken and chips, are almost universally available.

Stomach upsets are much more common when travelling. Wash fruit well and give your children sensible cooked food rather than exotic food from roadside stalls. Diarrhoea can be unpleasant and, if severe or prolonged, dangerous. Get advice from a local doctor, but sugary, milk-free drinks like cola are good substitutes for food in an emergency. They are also popular with children who just need fluid to tide them through the episode. Follow your doctor's advice about whether it is safe to let your child drink the local water. If in doubt, give him bottled water only.

Sunburn and sunstroke are constant threats in hot climates. A child's skin is usually paler than that of an adult, and does not filter out sunlight very effectively. Children tend to get burned badly, unless they are gradually exposed to the sun, and there is some evidence of a link between sunburn as a child and skin cancer as an adult. It's safest to cover them with lots of Factor 8 sunscreen, and make them wear a hat so that sunburn doesn't spoil their holiday.

Let your child make the most of his holiday, because for him, it will seem a very long time before the next one comes around. Encourage him to try everything that seems safe, because his holiday is an adventure, and he wants to have fun.

○ A beach holiday is ideal for children, as the sand, water and presence of other children provides plenty of interest.

Getting on with the Grandparents

Quite understandably, grandchildren are the apple of their grandparents' eyes, and they indulge the children at every opportunity. They can relive their own early parenthood, and for many it is fun to see a child develop without all the worries of being primarily responsible for him. Equally naturally, because they have brought up children themselves, they believe they know how a child should be treated. These two factors can combine to cause problems, and many parents resent their own parents 'interfering' in the upbringing of their children.

Holidays with grandparents

It is quite true that a long stay with grandparents who let a child do all the things which are discouraged at home can cause disruptions later on. But this kind of freedom can be accommodated by treating it as a holiday, during which the rules can be relaxed, and making it clear to the child that once he gets home, things will get back to normal. It is far more disruptive if a fond grandparent takes the child's side in a minor dispute at home; "Let him stay up a bit later", "Let me buy him some sweets", "Here's some money to buy yourself a treat" are all comments which are guaranteed to irritate a parent who discourages this sort of behaviour.

Interference or help?

It can be difficult to tell a grandparent politely, and without causing offence, that you know best, and that things have to be done the way you want them. Your own parents obviously think that *they* know best, and your patience and tact may be stretched to the utmost if you are to avoid an argument. But the fact remains that it's far better to clear the air and tell them how you want to run things than to seethe with frustration because things are not going how you want, and you don't like to offend by telling them. How you broach this tactfully depends entirely on your relationship with your or your partner's parents, but it is one area where you must stand firm, or you will find your child skillfully playing you off one against the other.

On the positive side, grandparents can be a great help to you, and a joy to your child. The majority of grandparents gladly tolerate a noisy, boisterous child, and can give you a welcome break which you can use to get on with other things. Don't forget that they may have got out of the habit of looking after children themselves, and though they enjoy playing with your child, they will be quite relieved when they can hand him back to you and resume their normal peaceful routine. It's not fair on them to leave a really unruly child in their care for a long time, particularly if they are elderly.

Death in the Family

Death is still a taboo subject, which most people find difficult to discuss directly. It is particularly difficult to talk to a child about someone's death when you feel forced to use euphemisms like 'Going to sleep' to avoid shocking or frightening the child. In fact, small children do not understand the concept of death, and are therefore not frightened by it directly, because they do not understand it's full implications. They will probably be disturbed at the sight of a very sick person, because they can see that something looks very wrong with them, but the actual death itself is less disturbing because they cannot identify with the situation.

○ A child may become frightened and clinging after the death of a close relative or friend.

For any family which keeps pets, death is an easier subject to broach. A child will readily recognize that an old cat or dog may be suffering, and that being put down is the best thing for them, although it is upsetting. Similarly, they usually greet the death of a pet hamster or gerbil with floods of tears, but forget all about it after a few days. Once they are over the initial shock, the ritual of a 'funeral' in the garden is a good way to help prepare them for the concept of death as it affects people.

If someone your child knows dies, after an illness, it is usually possible to prepare them by explaining how ill they are, and that they are not expected to get better. When someone dies suddenly, it is not so easy to provide an explanation.

What you actually say to the child depends largely on your religious beliefs. Children's curiosity almost always means that they will be interested in finding out what happens to a person after they die, both physically and spiritually, and you should answer their questions as honestly and openly as possible, consistent with your own beliefs. If you try to avoid the issue, you will make them feel that there is something to hide, and something to be feared.

After the death of a person whom your child knows well, he may have a few behavioural problems. Nightmares and bed-wetting are not uncommon, and indicate his level of anxiety about what has happened. His anxiety is probably due to his incomplete understanding of the death, and talking to him about it will help. He may also become more 'clingy', following you about in case you too disappear.

If your child seems to be very distressed, ask yourself the following questions.

Why is my child afraid of death?

○ Has he overheard whispered conversations, from which he has been excluded?

○ Is he under some misapprehensions because of disinformation he has heard from his friends?

○ Is he suffering from perfectly natural grief for someone he loves, which will gradually become less painful for him?

○ Have you tried too hard to shelter him from the reality of the situation, so he thinks that death is something to be feared?

○ Have you made it clear that nothing nasty is going to happen to him or you?

○ Does he feel in some way responsible?

Birthdays and Special Occasions

Birthdays and special occasions like Christmas, Diwali or Hannukah are a happy time for the whole family, and particularly for your child, who is generally the centre of attention. At the same time, you have the additional worry of buying presents and organizing parties.

Buying presents for a child between three and six is not difficult, apart from the cost. There is a huge choice of toys available, and many of these will appeal to your child. Don't be too impressed by the packaging, but think what he will actually do with the toy before you make your choice. Don't fall into the trap of concentrating on 'educational' toys which you hope will 'improve' your child. He wants to *play* with them, and if he educates himself at the same time, that's just a bonus. His preference for toys will be heavily influenced by his friends' possessions, and there are fashions for toys among quite young children. Similarly, constant exposure to television advertising may convince your child that he *must* have certain toys. Don't feel pressurized into buying expensive toys that you can't afford. At this age your child will have little understanding of money and will not care how much his present cost.

Parties

Your child will fit happily into a family party where he knows everyone, but you may find that he becomes overexcited. We have all seen children at a party become more and more excited and boisterous, followed by the inevitable tears. It's always best to distract children from their play if you see it getting out of hand, rather than hopefully telling them to "Calm down". Offering a snack or a drink may provide a welcome break and a change of mood.

If you organize a birthday party for your child, you will be faced with a lot of unfamiliar children, who will all behave in different ways. They won't all have the same table manners, and they certainly won't appreciate what you consider to be acceptable behaviour in your home. Similarly, they may dislike food which is your child's favourite. Nevertheless, with careful planning your party will be a roaring success.

One of the most important factors to consider is the size of the party. Try to avoid inviting the whole play group if possible. It is more difficult to supervise a large group of boisterous children than a small one, and you may not have the space to accomodate large numbers.

Parties

Don't make the mistake of thinking you have to come up with wildly original ideas for games and food. Children adore playing games that they know well and will not mind playing 'Pass the parcel' or 'Musical bumps' at every party. The most important

Traditional birthday tea parties are still popular with young children.

thing is to keep the time between games to a minimum. It is when they have nothing else to do that children will start getting into mischief or squabbling amongst themselves.

Party food

As far as party food is concerned, finger foods are the most suitable as children can then pick the bits they want to eat without creating lots of waste. You will probably find disposable plates and tablecloths a boon if you can afford them.

Tips for a child's party

○ Keep it short. That way the children won't get bored, and you won't get overtired.

○ Keep the food and drinks very simple, because young children don't have sophisticated tastes.

○ Make a list of games or entertainments which you can start them off with, but be prepared to change the routine if they don't seem interested.

○ With younger children, ask some of the parents to stay with you to help out. This can be useful if there are tears or accidents and a child needs comforting.

○ Make each child feel special by providing *small* presents for them to take home.

○ Make sure that arrangements have been made to collect all the children at the proper time.

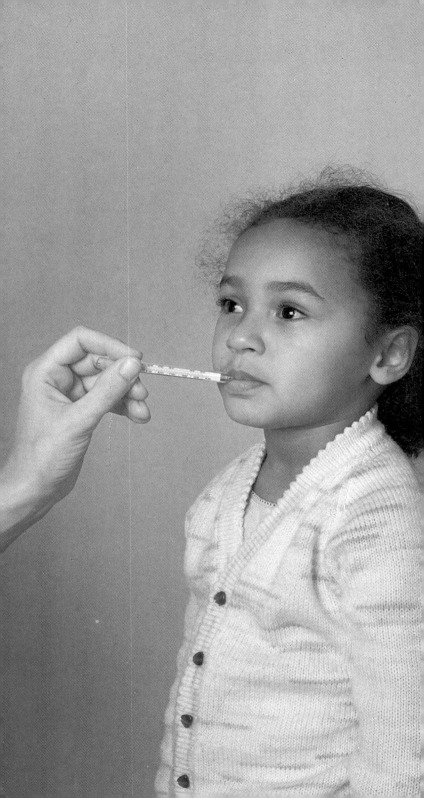

HEALTH AND SAFETY

Common-sense Safety

Every year, one in six of all children under five years old have to go to hospital because of an accident in their home. The home is a much more dangerous place than the road, though we rarely appreciate the hazards, because we are so used to them.

Danger in the home

You can never make your home totally safe, but you can eliminate a lot of the hazards if you remember that unlike an adult, a child's curiosity and wish to explore are not tempered with caution. So although you might not dream of tasting an anonymous liquid in an unlabelled bottle, a child will readily take an exploratory swig. In the same way she will poke sharp objects into live wall sockets, lean dangerously out of the window, and touch the fire to see if it is really hot. This is not because she is wilfully reckless; it is completely consistent with the way in which she learns about the other things in her environment. So it has to be *your* responsibility to keep her environment as safe as possible, without making it too restrictive.

Older children are not always aware of potential dangers for their younger playmates. Sitting on a wall or fence, for example, can lead to a nasty accident if the child topples backwards.

Danger outdoors

You can often supervise your child in the home, but when she plays out of doors, you may have to trust her to be sensible. Schools and playgrounds take reasonable precautions to protect children, but they cannot make allowances for unpredictable behaviour. If you think that your child is old enough to play without proper supervision, then you should be completely satisfied that you have explained to her all the possible hazards, and can trust her.

Safety tips for the home

○ Fix a fireguard around any room heater which could be hot enough to burn her.

○ Turn pan handles away from the front of the cooker, so hot pans cannot easily be pulled off.

○ Get some special clips to keep the cables from electric irons and kettles coiled tidily out of the way, so they won't trip up your child.

○ Fit child-proof covers on all electric sockets and explain to your child that she must never poke any objects into the sockets.

○ Don't leave your child unattended in the bath and don't let her run the hot water, in case she gets scalded.

○ Fit catches or safety chains on upstairs windows, so they won't open far enough for a child to lean out.

○ Make sure that safety glass is fitted in all inside glass doors and patio or conservatory doors.

○ Make sure your child tidies her toys away and discourage her from leaving anything at the top of the stairs where she might trip over.

○ Don't allow your child to walk around carrying sharp objects, or with glasses which could get smashed in a fall, or with sharp objects like pencils in her mouth.

○ Keep drugs and dangerous chemicals in *locked* cupboards. Don't underestimate a child's ability to climb up to apparently inaccessible cupboards and shelves.

○ Dispose of all plastic bags or store them where there is no danger of a child finding them and suffocating.

○ Discourage playing on the stairs.

○ Encourage your child to be responsible; explain to her why certain things can be dangerous.

If you have a garden, you should ensure that your child cannot slip out of a side gate or under a rickety fence without your knowledge. Remember that garden tools can also pose a serious threat to your child if she plays with them so do not leave forks, hoes and other implements lying around. When mowing the

awn, or using electric hedge cutters insist that she keeps at a safe
distance and never leave them running.

Children must also be protected from fireworks and bonfires.
Never let your child light fireworks herself or go to look at ones
that have been lit but not gone off.

A child's natural curiosity can lead him into danger, so matches
and other inflammables should be locked away.

Protecting your child outside the home

○ Never leave a child alone near water, even a paddling pool. Remember that water is like a magnet for a child, so take the sensible precaution of teaching her to swim as early as possible. Swimming classes for children are available in most areas. Fence off garden ponds securely.

○ Explain to your child that berries and fungi she finds outside could be poisonous.

○ Avoid growing poisonous plants in your garden.

○ Check that swings and other garden structures are assembled properly and do not become unsafe with use.

○ Keep all garden chemicals, such as weedkillers and pesticides, locked away where your child cannot find them.

○ If you let your child play unsupervised in the park or streets, explain to her the dangers of going off with strangers and insist that she always tells you where she is going.

When out in the dark or on a gloomy day wearing bright clothing or a reflective safety strip makes a child more visible to traffic.

Cars and roads

Even if you always accompany your child when she is out in the street, it is important to teach her to be aware of the danger traffic poses. As with most things, she will learn from the example you set so you must practice what you preach about where and when to cross the road.

If you have a car, your child should travel in the back seat in an approved car seat, or on a booster seat and restrained with a seat belt. If the car has child safety locks on the doors, use them.

○ Play can be so all-engrossing that children forget the danger posed by traffic.

Guidelines for road safety

○ When travelling in a car, remember that *all children travelling in the front passenger seat or the back of the car should wear safety belts or sit in a proper child car seat.* A child without restraints can suffer horrifying injuries in the event of an accident, and the cost of safety belts is a small price to pay to protect them. They must be properly fitted, exactly as recommended by the manufacturer.

○ Don't allow your child to play in the road. Her enthusiasm in running about and playing will overrule any road safety rules you have taught her.

○ Hold your child's hand when walking along the pavement, in case she decides to dash into the road. You cannot depend on a three-year-old to walk placidly at your side, as she may suddenly decide to investigate something which looks interesting.

○ Teach your child to cross the road safely, holding her hand, and explain what you are doing when you look out for traffic or wait for pedestrian signals.

○ Don't allow her to ride her tricycle or bicycle in the road.

Preparing a Child for Hospital

A hospital is very different from home, and it is a strange and frightening place for a child. If your child has to go into hospital she will already be feeling unwell, and that is frightening enough without all the strange faces and the unfamiliar situation.

You can prepare your child for going into hospital so that it won't be such an ordeal for her. It will still be difficult for you though, and the parents' own anxieties are one of the most important factors in causing a child's fear of hospital.

○ Nurses make special efforts to put sick children at ease.

First you need to find out exactly what is going to happen. Talk to the staff about anything that concerns you.

Questions to ask hospital staff

○ What sort of treatment will your child receive? You need to know this in order to explain it to her.

○ How much time can you spend with her? Many hospitals will allow parents unrestricted visiting, and some can make arrangements for you to stay overnight, if necessary.

○ Will she be in a large or small ward? Some children are frightened at being in a large ward where they feel 'lost'.

○ What sort of toilet arrangements will she have to use? Will she be able to use the lavatory, or will she be helped to use a bedpan?

○ What sort of state will she find herself in when she wakes up after an operation? If she will wake up with a drip attached, or tubes fitted, she needs to be warned about this well in advance.

○ What arrangements does the hospital make for children who are recovering? Are there play facilities, or will your child be expected to stay in or near her bed?

○ What sort of food will she be given? If your child is a picky eater, you will have to let the hospital know what she likes. Find out if there is a choice of food offered.

How you can help

Once you understand the situation yourself, you can prepare your child. There are some good children's books about hospitals which you can look at with your child. To get her used to the idea of hospital procedures play 'doctors and nurses' games with her, then explain to her what will be happening. Don't try to deceive her by saying "It won't hurt", when it would be more honest to say "It won't hurt much", or you may find her tearfully blaming you for her discomfort later on. If you make the point that it will be more uncomfortable for her if she doesn't go into hospital to have treatment than it would be to stay as she is, she can see the point of the treatment, and will not regard hospital as some form of exotic punishment you have dreamed up for her.

Let her take as many of her familiar things with her as is reasonably practicable. Favourite toys, books, and her own pyjamas will all help her to feel more secure in a strange environment.

Familiar toys and books will help a child feel more at home in hospital, especially when her parents cannot be with her.

Anaesthetics

If she needs an anaesthetic, try to be present when she starts to come round. In her confused state, she needs a familiar face to comfort her. If there are facilities for you to stay with her in hospital, make use of this to be with her as much as possible, so you can explain to her what is happening.

You must expect tears from any child in hospital. She is likely to blame you for what is happening to her, but she will still want you with her all the time. If you are only able to visit, she will almost certainly cry when you have to leave. Explain to her exactly when you will be back so that she doesn't feel abandoned. When she doesn't cry and seems very cheerful, you know that she is on the mend, and has made some friends in the hospital. Some children remain very quiet and subdued during their stay in hospital, and these are often the ones who are very frightened, and feel that they have been betrayed or even abandoned by their parents.

Emergencies

All this careful preparation is no help if your child is suddenly admitted to hospital because of an emergency. When this happens, you will have to insist on staying with her, because she will probably be terrified and confused, and will need someone familiar to cling to.

Once your child has settled down, and you can begin to think about getting her home again, tell her about what you have been doing, and how you have made her own room look nice for her. Find out from the medical staff exactly when she can be discharged, and what subsequent treatment she may need, and make sure you tell her as well, so she won't be upset if things are not quite as she had expected.

How do You Cope if You are Ill?

Parents with young children dread becoming ill. Being a parent is usually a full-time job, and it is often difficult enough when you are feeling healthy, let alone coping with an energetic child when you feel awful yourself. Unfortunately, a small child does not really understand illness, and she won't see why you want her to be extra quiet, or why she cannot have her meals at the usual time just because you feel unwell.

How you cope depends on how bad you feel and whether you have a partner. If you have an infection that is likely to clear up within a couple of days, your partner may be able to take time off to look after you and your child. Obviously if you have a cold or flu, you won't want to give it to your child, so you should keep away from her by staying in bed to avoid spreading the infection, so long as there is someone to care for her.

Friends and relatives can often help and will usually rally round to help with such things as meals for your child, collecting her from nursery school and looking after her until your partner gets home from work. It may be less trouble for her to go and stay with them than to expect people to keep popping in to make sure that everything is alright. Alternatively, you may need to have someone staying with you full time.

If you are seriously ill, and there is no-one to help, you must ask your doctor to involve the social services. He or she will be able to arrange for someone to call and decide how best to provide the help you need. Although social workers are sometimes overstretched, they will assist when help is essential.

○ A good relationship between doctor and child is important whether it is the child or parent who is sick.

Is Your Child Ill?

You will soon get to know your child's behaviour very well indeed, and parents almost always know that there is something wrong before it 'develops' to the point where a doctor can diagnose the problem. Now your baby is growing up, you will be less worried about minor health problems, because you will have seen how she can charge about happily while having a streaming cold, and because she is able to tell you how she feels.

Sometimes you may be in doubt about when to call the doctor, or whether to take your child to the surgery. There are some important points to look out for.

When to consult the doctor

Symptoms that need immediate attention

○ She is difficult to rouse, or seems not to recognize you.

○ Fits and convulsions.

○ When you suspect she may have swallowed something which could be harmful, or if she has pushed an object into her nose or ears.

Symptoms which could be serious

○ Diarrhoea and vomiting.

○ Refusal to eat.

○ Feels unusually hot or cold.

○ Coughing or spitting blood (in the absense of a nosebleed).

○ Severe earache.

○ Violent and continuous stomach aches.

○ Limbs and neck are floppy.

Surgery or home visits

Whenever possible you should take your child to the surgery but if your child is too ill phone to ask the doctor to visit her at home.

If you suspect that your child may have an infectious illness but she is well enough to be taken to the doctor's surgery, ring the receptionist in advance. You may be told to wait in a seperate area away from the other patients, or the doctor may prefer to make a home visit.

○ During convalescence a child will need to be kept fully occupied
while he is in bed.

Getting further advice

Once you have discussed a medical problem with the doctor, but your child still seems to be getting worse, don't hesitate to contact the doctor again. Even if he operates an appointments system, your doctor will probably have made allowances to see sick children without an appointment. If you can't get hold of the right person, then go straight to the accident and emergency department of your nearest hospital for help.

What to tell the doctor

Your family doctor should be the main source of help and treatment for your sick child. It will usually be quickest to take her to the doctor rather than waiting for him/her to visit you. Try to sort out in your own mind exactly what you think is wrong with your child, because the doctor won't know how she normally behaves, so he/she may not realize how much her behaviour has changed.

Nursing a sick child

A sick child can demand a lot of attention, and this can be a problem for working parents. She probably won't want to eat, but it is important that she still drinks plenty of fluids, though you may need to use some persuasion to get her to drink. Once she starts to feel a bit better, you will be able to persuade her to eat her favourite meals, but don't overload her with a huge plateful while she's still not feeling quite right.

Body temperatures tend to rise and fall quite fast in small children, and you will need to check her regularly. Keep her wrapped up and out of draughts, but don't bundle her up so much that you make her feel even more hot and sweaty. If she is hot and sticky, she will be comfortable if you change her sheets and pyjamas regularly. If she is likely to vomit, keep a clean bowl or a potty by the bed for her to use rather than having to rush to the toilet.

If your child is very sick, the doctor and health visitor will take special care of her, but for other children, it is best to let them decide what they want. If she insists on getting out of bed and running around, then it won't do her any harm, although you may find you have to put her back to bed for a rest again quite soon. She can usually rest just as well in a nest of cushions and blankets on the sofa, where she can see what is going on. Moving her around a bit will break the monotony of lying in bed.

If she is feeling really miserable, you will probably find that she prefers to be cuddled rather than going to bed, and it is normal for a sick child to become very clingy and weepy.

Buy or borrow lots of small toys and comics, so she feels that you are making a special fuss of her. These will also stop her getting bored, and she is less likely to make a fuss about having to stay in bed and rest.

A sick child should be encouraged to drink plenty of fluids.

Explain to her why she feels unwell, and how long it is likely to be before she feels better. She will understand "one week" or even "ten days", but "soon" is too vague a concept to grasp.

The sick child – points to watch

○ Keep her warmly wrapped up, and keep the room warm – but not too hot, or stuffy.

○ Treat for a raised temperature (see p.198).

○ Encourage her to have plenty of rest.

○ Give her lots to drink.

○ Keep her occupied once she starts to feel better.

Taking your child's temperature

For babies and very awkward or distressed toddlers a liquid crystal thermometer, or fever strip, may be used to take the temperature. However, mercury thermometers give a more accurate reading. You can now buy ones that emit a 'beep' when the mercury has finished rising.

At three years of age, a child is still too young to have her temperature taken orally as she risks a mouthful of glass and mercury should she bite the thermometer. Instead, get a reading by placing the thermometer in her armpit (see p.188).

By the time she is five or six years, you can place the thermometer under your child's tongue, but explain beforehand that she must not bite it. Do not leave her alone while the thermometer is in her mouth.

When taking a child's temperature using the underarm method, hold his arm still to prevent the thermometer becoming dislodged.

Whichever method you are using, first shake the thermometer sharply so that the mercury column falls to a point towards the beginning of the scale. Place the thermometer under the child's tongue or arm and leave for the amount of time specified in the manufacturer's instructions. Remove it, then tilt the glass until you can see the mercury column and read this off against the scale. (A healthy child's temperature will usually be 37–37.5°C/96.8°F but it will vary according to the time of day and how active she has been). Afterwards, wash the thermometer with cold water (hot might cause the glass to crack) and store in a safe place.

○ By six years a child is old enough to have her temperature taken orally, but she should not be left alone with the thermometer.

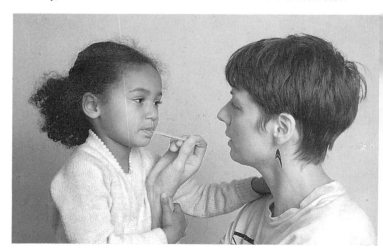

Dealing with Common Emergencies

Many kinds of medical emergencies affect young children and adults alike, and to deal with these properly you need a thorough grounding in first aid. There are several excellent books and courses which can inform you about this important subject. But there are a few medical problems and first aid techniques which are very specific to the health and safety of children, and everyone should be aware of how to deal with these situations. The most important are outlined below.

Burns and shocks

Burns can be caused by heat, excess sun, chemical or electric shock. Superficial burns, like sunburn, cause only redness, and can be treated with calamine lotion, but all other types of burn need proper medical attention. The basic treatment for all burns is to cool the area as fast as possible, by holding the affected part under cold running water for ten to 20 minutes. Do not try to pull clothing away from the area as you may tear the skin. Instead, soak the whole area. Then the burned area should be covered with a clean dry dressing or cloth, and the casualty taken immediately to the emergency department of the hospital for proper treatment. Apart from very small superficial burns, medical treatment is important to prevent later infection of the damaged skin.

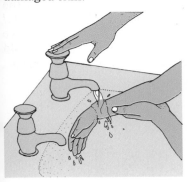

Cool the burnt area of skin by flooding it with cold running water.

Electric shocks are particularly dangerous, because the burn is often internal and may be much more serious than it first appears. If your child has received an electric shock, before you touch her you must make sure that it is safe to do so. If she is still in contact with the source of electricity, pull out the plug or switch it off. If you cannot do this, use something non-conducting, like a piece of wood, plastic or cardboard, to push them clear of the power.

The child may be unconscious, and will need immediate resuscitation (see p.193). This must be carried out immediately. Turn the child into the recovery position (see p.191), and get immediate medical assistance.

If the child's clothing is on fire, make him lie on the ground. Either douse the flames with a bucket of water or smother them with a (non-flammable) blanket.

FIRST AID – FOREIGN OBJECTS

Foreign objects

Choking is usually caused by inhaling foreign objects, but more commonly a child will insert an object, such as a bead or a sweet, into the ear or nose, where it becomes stuck.

Nose If your child has pushed something into her nose, she will probably be in some pain and distress. Do not attempt to remove the object; take her straight to hospital for expert attention.

Ear If your child has something in her ear, she will probably scratch and pull at her ear in an attempt to dislodge it. *Never* poke cotton wool buds into the ear to try and clear it, because you will only push the obstruction further in. If you think the obstruction could be an insect, try pouring some warm water into the ear, to see if it will float out. If not, you must take the child to hospital for treatment.

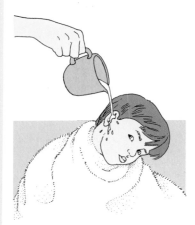

Pouring warm water into the ear may flush out an insect.

Choking

Blockage of the air passages caused by inhaling vomit, food or some other object is a serious medical emergency, and requires immediate and effective action.

The first aid technique varies according to the age of the child, but the one given here is suitable for children from three to six years.

1 Check in her mouth to see if you can remove the obstruction by hooking it out with your fingers. If this fails, administer back slaps (right).

2 Sit on a chair and lay the child over your knees, face down. Thump her firmly between the shoulder blades up to four times, using the flat of your hand.

3 If the obstruction is still not removed sit her up on your lap, facing forwards, and clasp one arm round her abdomen, with your fist clenched and thumb towards her. Now press your clenched fist sharply inwards, moving it up and inwards, and repeat the action firmly until the obstruction is ejected.

4 If she is unconscious, turn her into the recovery position. Lay her face down, and draw up one knee and arm on the same side, so she is lying partly on her side. Turn her head to face the same side, tilting the head back and pushing the jaw forward to keep the air passages open. *Get medical help immediately*.

Fits

Fits or convulsions are not uncommon in young children, and are most common in children under the age of three, although they can still occur later. These fits are usually the result of a rise in body temperature, and they are called febrile convulsions. A child's brain is more sensitive to the effects of high temperature than an adult, and the brain reacts by sending random signals to the muscles of the body. The result is that the child becomes stiff and unconcious, with the whole body twitching and the jaws clenched shut. She may also pass urine and faeces.

Because a fit is very frightening, it is natural to try and do something to help. In fact, there is not very much that can be done, and the fit usually stops of its own accord quite quickly. If it is a febrile convulsion, then the child will be very hot and sweaty, and can be sponged down to lower the temperature. The most serious immediate risk is of inhaling vomit, so you must turn the child face down, with the head to one side, loosening her clothing to help her breathing. Move her into a clear space so she doesn't hurt herself by banging against the furniture, and *never* try to force her mouth open.

As soon as the fit is over, the child will be in an exhausted sleep. Until this point you must stay with her all the time in case she chokes (see p.191), but when the fit has passed, turn her into the recovery position (see opposite) and *get medical assistance immediately*.

If the problem was a febrile convulsion, you may need to take care not to let her get overheated again; however, this condition usually clears up as she gets older. There are many other causes of fits and so it is always important to seek medical advice, particularly when it occurs for the first time.

Poisoning

Poisoning is among the most common domestic emergencies affecting children. There are very many items around your home which could poison a child, and others she may come across when she plays out of doors. Bleach, detergents, lavatory cleaner and kettle de-scaler are all very poisonous, and could be swallowed by an inquisitive toddler. In the garden, poisonous seeds, garden chemicals and toadstools are hazards. Many of these items cause internal burns when they are swallowed.

If your child drinks or eats *any* suspect substance, try to find out exactly what it was. In any case, make her drink lots of milk or water to dilute the poison, but *do not* try to make her vomit. If the child is unconscious, turn her into the recovery position (see opposite), and be prepared to resuscitate her if her breathing is affected. You must wash her mouth thoroughly before attempting mouth-to-mouth resuscitation, to protect your own mouth from possible corrosive substances. *Get medical help urgently*. Remember to tell the emergency team what she has taken.

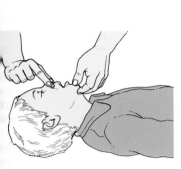

1 Lay the child on a hard surface. Remove any vomit or debris from his mouth with your fingers. Open his airway by tilting his head back slightly. Support his jaw with your other hand and pull his jaw forward, thereby extending his neck.

2 Check for breathing by putting your hand on his chest and listening with your ear near his mouth. If not, completely cover his mouth with yours and hold his nose. Breathe out gently, and watch to see if his chest expands. Allow the air out by taking your mouth away.

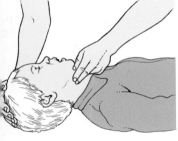

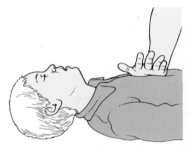

3 After the first three inflations, check that his heart is still beating by feeling the pulse along his carotid artery. Do this by sliding two fingers into the groove between his windpipe and the muscle in his neck, and feel gently for the pulse.

4 If the heart has stopped beating, you must immediately start heart massage. Use the heel of one hand to press over the lower breast bone to a depth of 2.5–3.5cm (1–1½in). Give 15 compressions to two ventilations, and after four cycles check the pulse. If still absent repeat, aiming for four cycles per minute.

5 Ideally there should be two people to carry out resuscitation – one to do mouth-to-mouth, and the other to do heart massage. If there are two of you, massage the heart five times and then inflate the lungs once. Repeat until the heart starts beating and the child is breathing. Then turn the child into the recovery position (see p.191) and get medical help urgently.

Coping with Minor Health Problems

Just like adults, children will inevitably suffer from minor ailments from time to time. In addition, they are likely to get fair amount of bumps and bruises as they energetically explore and play.

Bruises

These are the most common form of injury in children, an although they sometimes look very nasty, they seldom cause rea problems. They are caused by bleeding of very small bloo vessels, causing a discoloration under the skin. Bruises ar caused by a knock or a fall, but as children have slightly flexibl bones, there is unlikely to be a break even with the most sever bruising. The worst result from even bad bruising is likely to b pain and tenderness, and sometimes stiffness for a few days Most bruises are minor and do not cause any trouble at all.

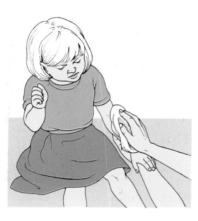

A cold compress applied to the site of the injury may reduce the bruising.

Apply a cold compress as soon as the child has been hurt. This can simply be cold water on a towel, or ice cubes wrapped in a towel. This may reduce the extent of the bruising. If the bruise is very painful, give paracetamol syrup at the specified dosage for the child's age.

In bad bruising, resting the affected part is usually recommended, but in a child, this problem usually sorts itself out, because if it hurts, she won't want to run about on it.

Grazes

Bruises are often accompanied by grazed skin, and dirt can enter and cause infection. Grazes need to be carefully washed, using mild diluted antiseptic solution, then left exposed to the air until a scab has formed. If you apply a dressing, the weeping skin surface may stick to it and be painful to remove. If the wound does not dry up in an hour or so, or if it becomes red and puffy, get proper medical treatment.

○ A plaster will keep a cut or graze free from dirt.

Cuts

If your child cuts herself, you must first check to make sure that no dirt or other foreign bodies are in the wound. Rinse it under the tap, and remove any dirt, then cover it with some clean cloth or gauze and apply light pressure for two to three minutes. The bleeding will usually stop as the blood clots; if not, reapply the pressure until it does. Then you can cover the wound with an adhesive plaster, pulling the edges of the cut together to keep it closed. If the cut cannot be closed in this way, it may need stitching, and you should consult the doctor or nearest casualty department. Any deep or dirty cut may need a protective tetanus injection; ask your doctor if this is necessary.

Sore throat

Most sore throats are caused by virus infections, and are minor infections which clear up quickly. A few are caused by bacterial infections, and these may need treatment with antibiotics. If you look down the child's throat, and it is only reddened, then it is probably not a serious infection, but if there are white patches together with swollen glands in the neck, you should take her to the doctor.

In general, most sore throats in children can be treated with paracetamol every four hours, at the proper dosage for their age. Encourage her to drink plenty of liquids and do not try to persuade her to eat if she doesn't feel like it. Consult the doctor if the sore throat persists for several days, or if it seems to be getting worse. You must also seek medical attention if earache develops.

It is important for a child with a sore throat to keep drinking. If he finds opening his mouth is painful, give him a straw.

Coughs and sneezes

When the air passages are irritated or blocked, coughing or sneezing are the natural response of the body. They are reflexes which are intended to dislodge or expel anything obstructing the free flow of air. Sometimes the coughing or sneezing is caused by irritation resulting from an infection, and the child may cough and sneeze for a long time, becoming tired and irritable. The most troubling aspect of a cough is that it can wake a child from sleep.

Cough medicines can help, but the proper type must be given and always at the dosage recommended for the child's age. If the child has a phlegmy cough, an expectorant cough mixture should be given. This will encourage her to cough up the phlegm which is blocking her air passages. On the other hand, if she has a dry irritable cough, then a sedative cough mixture will help. Ask the pharmacist for advice before you buy cough medicine, as giving the wrong type would only make the cough worse.

Runny noses

Many small children seem always to have runny noses, sometimes because their parents have not taught them to blow or wipe their noses properly. If they suffer from colds or hay fever, a runny nose can be a real nuisance, and the nostrils become red and sore. Sometimes the nose becomes blocked, and the child is distressed at being forced to breathe through her mouth. Use vapour rub on the chest to ease the symptoms of a runny or congested nose, although the relief may only be temporary.

Runny noses are usually very temporary, and clear up when the underlying condition that has caused them gets better.

Vomiting

Vomiting happens when the stomach lining becomes irritated, either because of an infection, or by eating or drinking too much or the wrong things. Vomiting is simply the body's way to get rid of something which doesn't agree with it. Children often vomit very easily, and having emptied their stomach, they frequently feel much better. Vomiting is very common during infections such as tonsillitis and ear infections, or whenever they have a high temperature. Sometimes excitement or emotional stress can also cause vomiting.

After vomiting, don't try to persuade your child to eat anything for a while, and encourage her to sip small amounts of water. She will need to wash her mouth out to remove the unpleasant taste after vomiting. When she seems to be back to normal and feels hungry again, give her simple foods like biscuits or bread in small amounts to see if she can keep it down, before resuming a normal diet.

Take your child to the doctor if the vomiting is followed by continuing stomach pains, if it goes on for more than a day, if it is accompanied by diarrhoea or if the child also has a high temperature (above 38°C/100°F).

Diarrhoea

Diarrhoea can be caused by a number of things. In a child, it is sometimes the result of a change of diet, or of anxiety. A child who is worried about going to a new school sometimes has diarrhoea, or she may get it after trying a new food. Most types of diarrhoea are caused by an infection which irritates the bowel and causes food to pass through too quickly. This type of diarrhoea may happen if you go abroad for your holiday, and encounter infections which are different to those which are common at home, and which seldom cause problems there.

Sometimes there are warning stomach pains before diarrhoea, and there may also be some vomiting.

Although there are several medicines which can be taken to treat diarrhoea, the best treatment is simply to miss out the next few meals, and drink nothing but clear fluids (sugary drinks with no milk) for a while. (Cola is particularly good in an emergency.) It is very important to drink plenty of fluid to avoid dehydration, and special anti-dehydration compounds are available from the chemist. Ask the pharmacist for advice about these. The condition should clear up spontaneously within a day, but if not, seek medical attention promptly, especially if your child is or recently has been abroad.

Common Childhood Infections

A number of infections and complaints are particularly associated with childhood, including chickenpox and eczema. Once your child is in regular contact with other children at nursery or school she is almost certain to catch some infections.

Colds

Young children seem to catch cold after cold, and it is not unusual for a child to have five or six really unpleasant colds each year. Once they start to mix with other children at nursery or infant schools they are exposed to even more infections, and will experience further bouts of colds. Colds are caused by viruses, and there is no real treatment other than giving paracetamol syrup to keep the temperature down. They seldom last for more than a week, but they can often lead to other infections when they weaken the resistance. Catarrh and bacterial tonsillitis can follow a bad cold.

Many young children become distressed when their nose is blocked by mucus, because they find it uncomfortable to breathe only through the mouth. If your child has not yet learned to blow her nose effectively, you can wipe away this mucus, but you should not try to clear it by pushing tissue or cotton wool buds into the nostrils. It may be worth smearing some medicated rub around the nostrils and on the upper chest, as this can help to clear the nose. Try to teach your child to blow or wipe her nose.

Warning

Aspirin has been used to control fevers in children, but it is now known that aspirin can be very dangerous to them, so it should on no account be used in children under the age of 12 years.

Fevers

A high temperature occurs in almost all infections and, in young children especially, this can make them feel wretched and bad tempered. The fever is not in itself dangerous, but if it gets too high in a younger child it can sometimes cause a fit or febrile convulsion, when she becomes rigid and shakes (see p.192). This is a medical emergency which needs immediate treatment.

Usually a fever causes little more than discomfort and disturbed rest in a child. There are several ways you can make your child more comfortable. Sponging with lukewarm water will help to cool her down, as will a cool damp cloth applied to her forehead. However, the cooling effects are only temporary. A fever-reducing drug like paracetamol syrup in a special paediatric form is the most effective way to bring down the temperature and keep it down.

Chickenpox

Almost all young children catch chickenpox, as it is very contagious. Infection usually follows when the child starts to mix with other children at a play group or nursery. The disease is probably contagious before the characteristic spots appear, and by then it may be too late to isolate the infected child from others. Your child will be infectious for one week after the appearance of the rash or four days after the last crop. Chickenpox often starts with a fever, but this may not occur. An itchy rash appears first, followed by small red spots which develop into tiny blisters (see p.200). The rash usually starts on the body, then spreads over the face and limbs. The incubation period for chickenpox (the time between infection and the appearance of symptoms) is between ten to 21 days, averaging about 15 days.

Chickenpox is seldom serious in children, and the only real problem it causes is scratching at the itchy spots, which can cause scarring. Keep your child's fingernails very short while she is itchy, and treat the spots with calamine lotion. A sedative may be prescribed by the doctor if the itching is so bad that the child cannot sleep.

Rubella

Rubella or German measles is a viral disease, like chickenpox. It starts off with a fever, followed a couple of days later by a rash and pale flat spots (see p.200). These first appear behind the ears and around the temples, then spread over the rest of the body. The glands in the neck are usually swollen, especially at the back of the neck. Rubella is usually a very mild infection, and many children have it without their parents being aware that anything is wrong. But it is very dangerous to unborn babies in the womb of mothers who have never had the infection. For this reason, rubella immunization is important for all girls. The incubation period is from 14 to 19 days and the child is contagious for seven days from the onset of the rash.

Measles

Measles is a dangerous infection, is extremely contagious and sometimes leads to serious aftereffects. There are serious attempts to eradicate measles, and it is now a notifiable disease, which your doctor must report to the health authorities. When it does occur, measles starts off with cold-like symptoms, progressing to a cough and a very high temperature. When the temperature peaks, the rash soon appears as clusters of small bright red spots on the neck and around the ears, gradually spreading over the whole body (see p.200). The incubation period is 12 to 14 days, but cold-like symptoms may appear earlier. Keep your child isolated for seven days after the appearance of the rash but your child may have been infectious for a few days prior to the appearance of the rash.

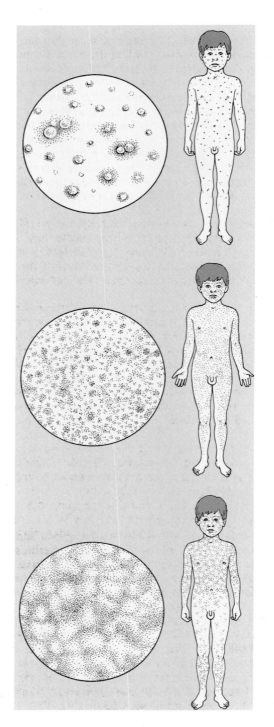

As chickenpox develops the red spots become blisters, mainly affecting the trunk and face. If they are scratched they may leave permanent scars.

The rash of rubella (German measles) is characterized by pale, flat spots that merge into larger patches.

The measles rash starts around the neck and behind the ears and then spreads over the body as irregular red blotches.

Mumps

Mumps causes characteristic facial swelling and the symptoms are quite clear. The glands in one or both sides of the face swell, and so may the glands under the chin. The child will be feverish, thirsty, and may have a stiff neck. Mumps usually clears up quickly, without complications. The incubation period can be between 14 to 28 days, but the symptoms usually appear after 17 to 18 days. Keep the child isolated for nine days after the onset of the swelling.

Worms

Worm infections of the intestines are very common in children, and are often picked up when children begin to play together. Worm eggs leave the body of an infected person in their faeces, and spread to another person when they are taken in through the mouth. This happens when there is poor toilet hygiene, and a child has not wiped herself properly, or has failed to wash her hands. Some types of worm deposit their eggs on the skin around the anus, so a child can easily reinfect herself if she scratches her bottom.

Scratching and irritation around the bottom and groin are the usual symptoms, and may be severe enough to keep a child awake at night. Fortunately, the treatment is simple and sure. If you suspect that your child may have picked up worms, ask the doctor or nurse for advice, and get the condition treated promptly. If you spot worms in the child's stool take them to the doctor so they can be identified and the correct treatment given. If you have other children, it is best to have all of them treated together, in case they have infected each other.

Nits and scabies

Although they are caused by different organisms, these conditions are similar in some respects. Nits are the egg sacs of tiny insect-like lice that live in the hair. Lice are almost invisible, and cling to the hair, feeding on blood and making the scalp itchy. The nits, or egg sacs, are sticky white objects like small grains of rice, which adhere to the hair. Infections are easily caught when children play together. They are absolutely nothing to do with dirt, and lice actually thrive on clean, well-groomed long hair.

Scabies is caused by similar tiny creatures, which burrow along just under the skin. They cause raised red tracks, often on the hands, and these itch intensely.

Both lice and scabies are easily treated by lotions which are applied to the scalp or to the affected skin. Ask the doctor or nurse to advise you on the best type to use.

Hay fever

Allergy to pollen is very common, but takes some time to develop, so it usually appears in older children. Hay fever is caused when the body reacts strongly against pollen grains that are inhaled, but similar conditions can also be caused by breathing in household dust, dust from animal hairs or feathers, or a wide range of other common substances.

Most parents at first confuse hay fever with a cold as the symptoms are often similar. It can cause red and weeping eyes, an itching and runny nose, and uncontrollable sneezing. There are several drugs available which can control hay fever very effectively, and unlike some earlier treatments, these will not make your child sleepy. If your child seems to be getting 'summer colds', or is often sneezing for no apparent reason, ask your doctor to check to see if this is caused by an allergy.

Eczema

This is an allergic skin condition which tends to run in families. It is quite common in children who will later develop hay fever or asthma. It causes red scaly patches, mostly on moist creases of the body, such as the groin and the creases at the back of knees and elbows. These patches often itch acutely, and the child is likely to scratch and cause the patches to become infected.

Eczema often flares up after an emotional upset, or when a child is stressed in some way. New situations such as a change of house, or going to a new school can often upset an affected child and make her eczema worse.

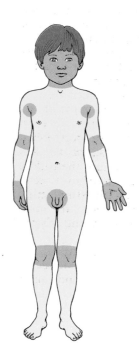

Eczema most commonly affects the face and neck, armpits, elbows, hands, groin and knees.

Treatment of eczema is difficult, but avoid putting your child into scratchy clothes which make the itching worse – 100 per cent cotton is best. Avoid the use of perfumed bubble baths or medicated soaps, which can irritate the inflamed skin.

Your doctor is the best person to help. Initially aqueous cream or emulsifying ointment will be tried. High concentration steroid creams can be dangerous and should only be prescribed by a doctor when it is actually necessary. Eczema usually clears up on its own, as the child gets older.

An asthmatic child will soon learn how to use an inhaler and should be able to participate fully in a normal active life.

Asthma

Asthma is related to hay fever in some ways. It is caused when the body reacts to some outside circumstance, such as breathing in dust, or to stress or excitement, by releasing a substance that causes the airways leading to the lungs to contract. This restricts the flow of air in and out and makes it difficult to breathe, producing an asthma attack. During an asthma attack, a child becomes very distressed, fighting for breath and wheezing.

Asthma attacks can be treated effectively, and often prevented by modern drugs. These are usually given in an inhaler, and even quite young children can be trained to use these properly when they feel an attack coming on. If your child has asthma, she will usually be treated at a hospital clinic at first, where she will be shown how to use an inhaler. She will also be shown how to cope if she does have an asthmatic attack. A child with asthma must always have access to her inhaler, and when she goes to school, the teachers will need to be advised of the situation, and what to do if she has an attack.

Later on, your family doctor usually takes over the treatment. When it is properly controlled, asthma does not usually cause lasting problems, and many children grow out of the condition as they get older.

Vaccinations

Effective immunization is available to protect your child against some common childhood infections as well as the most dangerous diseases:

○ Whooping cough
○ Diphtheria
○ Tetanus
○ Polio
○ Rubella
○ Mumps
○ Measles
○ Tuberculosis
○ Meningitis (some forms only).

Immunization has sometimes been criticized because, like any other form of medical treatment, there can be occasions when things go wrong. But if you offset the very small amount of risk against the former death toll from diseases like whooping cough and polio, the risk becomes worthwhile. It is only because so many children are immunized as a matter of course that these diseases are becoming more rare, and with most of the

Immunization timetable

Age	Immunization
3 months	Whooping cough Diphtheria Tetanus Polio (by mouth)
$4\frac{1}{2}$–5 months	Whooping cough Diphtheria Tetanus Polio (by mouth)
$8\frac{1}{2}$–11 months	Whooping cough Diphtheria Tetanus Polio (by mouth)
About 15 months	Measles Mumps Rubella
Preschool (around 4–5 years)	Diphtheria (booster) Tetanus (booster) Polio (booster) MMR (Measles, Mumps, Rubella for children who did not have it earlier)

immunizations, they will be immune for life afterwards. Talk to your doctor or health visitor about the benefits of immunization if you have any worries about it.

There are occasionally side effects after an immunization, such as a small red mark at the site of the injection, and young children may be feverish and irritable for the evening after. They can usually be soothed with paracetamol syrup, but if you think that any more serious side effects are developing you must tell your doctor immediately.

The age when immunizations can be given varies slightly, but that given below is usually followed. Further boosters will also be needed at a later date. In addition, vaccination against tuberculosis and some forms of meningitis may be offered to children who are considered to be at risk. Your doctor or health visitor will give you more details.

○ Medicine should always be given using a proper measuring spoon to ensure an exact dosage.

Drugs and Medicines

With the exception of aspirin (see p.198), the drugs administered to children between the ages of three and six years are the same as those given to adults, although the dosage is different. There is therefore no need to keep a supply of drugs especially for your child. Moreover, most drugs given to children will be prescribed by the doctor for treating specific medical conditions and you should be extremely cautious about giving any other, non-prescribed medicines.

Giving medicine to children has never been easier as nowadays the majority do not taste unpleasant, so there is no need to try to disguise them. It is extremely important that the correct dosage is given, and that if a course of antibiotics has been prescribed the complete course is given even if the child appears to have recovered. This is because the infection may not have been completely destroyed and could therefore reappear.

If the doctor has prescribed ear drops, tilt the child's head towards the unaffected side. Then position the dropper over (but not touching) the ear and release the drops.

Tips for the safe usage of medicines

○ Keep all medicines locked away from children.

○ Give the prescribed dosage of medicine, using the correct measuring spoon if applicable.

○ Don't keep medicines beyond the expiry date.

○ Do not give your child any medicines that have been prescribed to anyone else.

USEFUL ADDRESSES

There are numerous national organizations and self-help groups concerned with childcare and parental support. The list given here is limited to the more general ones. If your child has a specific handicap, your local doctor or health centre should be able to advise you on relevant organizations.

When writing to any of these organizations, enclose a stamped addressed envelope for your reply.

FAMILY LIFE
Gingerbread
35 Wellington Street,
London WC2E 7BN
Tel: (01) 240 0953
Local self-help groups offering support and encouragement for one-parent families.

Hyperactive Children's Support Group
71 Whyke Lane, Chichester,
West Sussex PO19 2LD
Tel: (0903) 725182 (9.30–3.30)
Information and advice for parents of suspected hyperactive children.

National Association for Maternal & Child Welfare (NAMCW)
1 South Audley Street,
London W1Y 6JS
Tel: (01) 493 2601. Education department: (01) 491 1315
Information and courses on child care at all levels.

National Council for One Parent Families
255 Kentish Town Road,
London NW5 2LX
Tel: (01) 267 1361 (Mon–Fri, except Wed, 10–2, 2–4)
Advice line and information service for lone parents. Library visits by appointment.

Parentline – OPUS
106 Godstone Road,
Whyteleafe CR3 0EB
Tel: (01) 645 0469
(or 01-645 0505 after hours)
Confidential telephone line manned by parents for parents experiencing problems.

BEREAVEMENT
Compassionate Friends
6 Denmark Street,
Bristol BS1 5DQ
Tel: (0272) 292778
Organization of bereaved parents offering support to other bereaved families.

Foundation for the Study of Infant Deaths
15 Belgrave Square,
London SW1X 8PS
Tel: (01) 235 0965
Raises funds for research. Personal support to bereaved families by phone, letter or local groups.

HANDICAPS
Contact a Family
16 Strutton Ground,
London SW1P 2HP
Tel: (01) 222 2695
Links families who have different disabilities or special needs through self-help groups.

In Touch
10 Norman Road,
Sale, Cheshire M33 3DF
*Voluntary organization to put
parents 'in touch' with other
parents whose children have the
same condition (no matter how
rare).*

**Voluntary Council for
Handicapped Children**
8 Wakley Street,
Islington, London EC1V 7QE
Tel: (01) 278 9441
*Comprehensive information and
advisory service covering all
aspects of childhood disabilities for
statutory and voluntary agencies,
professionals and parents.*

CHILDCARE AND PLAY
**National Childminding
Association**
8 Masons Hill, Bromley,
Kent BR2 9EY
Tel: (01) 464 6164
*Information for child minders and
parents on preschool care.*

**National Association for the
Welfare of Children in
Hospital (NAWCH)**
Argyle House,
29–31 Euston Road,
London NW1 2SD
Tel: (01) 833 2041
AWCH Scotland
Mrs Julia Millar,
15 Smith's Place,
Edinburgh EN6 8NT
Tel: (031) 553 6553
AWCH Wales
Mrs Anne Williams,
4 Chestnut Avenue,
West Cross,
Swansea SA3 5NL
Tel: (0792) 404232
*Supports sick children and their
families, and works to ensure that
health services are provided for
them.*

**Pre-school Playgroups
Association (PPA)**
61–63 King's Cross Road,
London WC1X 9LL
Tel: (01) 833 0991
Scottish PPA
14 Elliot Place,
Glasgow G3 8EP
Tel: (041) 221 4148
Northern Ireland PPA
11 Wellington Park,
Belfast DT9 6DJ
Tel: (0232) 662825
Wales PPA
2A Chester Street,
Wrexham,
Clwyd LL13 8BD
Tel: (0978) 358195
*The largest provider of pre-school
provision with some 18,000 groups
in England, Wales, Scotland,
Northern Ireland and overseas,
attended by 800,000 children.
Parental involvement welcomed.*

**Play Matters (National Toy
Libraries Association)**
68 Churchway,
London NW1 1LT
Tel: (01) 387 9592
*Information service on libraries
that lend toys; advice and training
on setting up toy libraries.*

**Working Mothers'
Association**
77 Holloway Road,
London N7 8JZ
Tel: (01) 700 5771
*Information for working parents
about childcare, plus support
through local groups.*

Australian Addresses

Association of Child Care Centres
1 Burwood Road,
Hawthorn, VIC 3122
Tel: (03) 819 1311

Association for the Welfare of Children in Hospital
2 King William Road,
North Adelaide, SA 5006
Tel: (08) 267 7347

Australian Early Childhood Association Inc.
Knox Street, Watson, ACT 2602
Tel: (062) 41 6900

Australian Multiple Birth Association (QLD)
10 Wordsworth Street,
Strathpine, QLD 4500
Tel: (07) 205 3816
Also, 18 Kandella Street,
Malvern East, VIC 3135
Tel: (03) 885 5300

Australian Parents Council Incorporated
PO Box 272,
N. Sydney, NSW 2060
Tel: (02) 92 7091

Babysitting Association of South Australia
Western Branch Road,
Woodside, SA 5244
Tel: (08) 389 7293

Canberra One Parent Family Support – Birthright
First Floor, Griffin Centre,
Canberra City, ACT 2601
Also, PO Box 685,
Civic Square, ACT 2608
Tel: (62) 47 4282

Child Accident Prevention Foundation of Australia
College of Surgeons Gardens,
26 Liverpool Street,
Melbourne, VIC 3000
Tel: (03) 663 1319

Child Health Association
Loinah Road,
Montagu Bay, TAS 7018
Tel: (002) 44 1355

Children's Activity Groups Association
150 Ennoggera Terrace,
Paddington, QLD 4064
Also, PO Box 382,
Paddington, QLD 4064
Tel: (07) 369 0572

Compassionate Friends
381 Pitt Street,
Sydney, NSW 2000
Tel: (02) 267 6962

Contact Children's Services
66 Albion Street,
Surry Hills, NSW 2010
Tel: (02) 212 4144

Council for Single Mothers and their Children
237 Flinders Street,
Melbourne, VIC 3000
Tel: (03) 654 7211

Dial-a-Mum of Australia
Palmerston Road,
Hornsey, NSW 2067
Tel: (02) 477 6777

Free Kindergarten Association of Victoria Inc.
383 Church Street,
Richmond, VIC 3121
Tel: (03) 428 3569

Gifted and Talented Children's Association of Western Australia
PO Box 186,
W. Perth, WA 6005
Tel: (09) 321 4821

Royal Society for the Welfare of Mothers and Babies
2 Shaw Street,
Petersham, NSW 2049
Tel: (02) 568 3633

FURTHER READING

Keep Your Baby Safe, Jane Asher (Penguin) 1988.

The Hyperactive Child, Barnes and Colquhoun (Thorsons) 1984.

Getting Ready for School, Margaret Basham (Longman) 1988.

Child Health, Prof. David Baum (Viking) 1989.

Good Mouthkeeping, John Besford (Oxford University Press) 1984.

Living with a Toddler, Brenda Crowe (Unwin Paperbacks) 1982.

First Aid Manual, (Dorling Kindersley) 1987.

My Child Won't Sleep, Jo Douglas and Naomi Richman (Penguin) 1984.

Solve Your Child's Sleep Problems, Dr Richard Ferber (Dorling Kindersley) 1985.

A Good Start; Healthy Eating in the First Five Years, Louise Graham (Penguin) 1986.

Birth to Five, Health Education Authority (Harper & Row) 1989.

The Development of the Young Child, Ronald S. Illingworth (Churchill Livingstone) 1987.

Fatherhood, Brian Jackson (Allen & Unwin) 1984.

The First Five Years, Hugh Jolly (Pagoda) 1984.

The Crying Baby, Sheila Kitzinger (Viking) 1989.

Baby and Child; From Birth to Age Five, Penelope Leach (Penguin) 1977.

My Child Won't Eat, Elizabeth Morse (Penguin) 1988.

From Birth to Five Years; Children's Developmental Progress, Mary D. Sheridan (NFER-Nelson) 1988.

The Mothercare Guide to Child Health, Dr Penny Stanway (Conran Octopus) 1988.

The Baby and Child Medical Handbook, Dr Miriam Stoppard (Dorling Kindersley) 1986.

The Baby Care Book, Dr Miriam Stoppard (Dorling Kindersley) 1983.

The Right Food for Your Kids, Louise Templeton (Century) 1984.

Living with a Hyperactive Child, Miriam Wood (Souvenir) 1984.

INDEX

ACKNOWLEDGEMENTS

The author and publishers would like to thank the following for their help in the preparation of this book:

Bradmore Park Kids Workshop, Daniel Hughes, Hannah Nicholas, Emily Furiel, Cleo Maynard, Sam Raeburn, Alison and Richard Woodley and their parents for allowing us to photograph them for artwork reference; also Saskia Frerichs, Hannah, Cleo, Richard and Alison for the drawings on pp. 17, 29 and 20; Coral Mula and Mary Tomlin for the illustrations; Peter Barber for the index; and Karen Temple for her practical advice and detailed comment on the text.

Photographic acknowledgements
The publishers would like to thank the following for kindly supplying photographs for this book:

Page 1 ZEFA; 6 Brian Ward; 8 Timothy Woodcock; 13 Betty Rawlings; 15 Lesley Howling; 23 ZEFA; 24 Courtesy, Allan Industries Ltd; 28 Lesley Howling; 33 Lesley Howling; 39 David Phillips; 40 Lesley Howling; 44 Lesley Howling; 48 Lesley Howling; 49 ZEFA; 53 Terry Woodley; 55 Terry Woodley; 58 Terry Woodley; 60 Lesley Howling; 61 ZEFA; 63 Lesley Howling; 67 Terry Woodley; 68 The Hutchison Library; 70 Timothy Woodcock; 76 Jennie Woodcock; 83 Timothy Woodcock; 90 ZEFA; 94 Timothy Woodcock; 97 The Hutchison Library; 99 ZEFA; 100 Jennie Woodcock; 102 Lesley Howling; 104 Lesley Howling; 109 Lesley Howling; 111 ZEFA; 113 Lesley Howling; 114 Lesley Howling; 117 Irene Windridge; 118 ZEFA; 120 Betty Rawlings; 122 David Phillips; 123 Lesley Howling; 124 Jennie Woodcock; 129 Jennie Woodcock; 131 Timothy Woodcock; 132 Timothy Woodcock; 135 Jennie Woodcock; 136 ZEFA; 142 Jennie Woodcock; 145 National Deaf Children's Society; 146 ZEFA; 148 Jennie Woodcock; 151 ZEFA; 154 ZEFA; 156 ZEFA; 157 ZEFA; 165 Timothy Woodcock; 166 Terry Woodley; 168 Lesley Howling; 170 Lesley Howling; 174 Lesley Howling; 177 Jennie Woodcock; 179 ZEFA; 180 ZEFA; 183 ZEFA; 185 Lesley Howling; 188 Lesley Howling; 195 Lesley Howling; 205 ZEFA.

Cover: ZEFA

Picture Research: Elaine Willis.